ADOBE AND IRON

The Story of the Arizona Territorial Prison

By JOHN MASON JEFFREY

1969

PROSPECT AVENUE PRESS, LA JOLLA, CALIFORNIA

Printed in The United States of America by Grant Dahlstrom
Pasadena, California

NOTE

IN THE long and colorful history of Yuma, the Arizona Territorial Prison is a famous landmark. Now a State Park, the partial ruins stand triumphantly on Prison Hill, overlooking the city of Yuma, in mute testimony of pioneer determination for law and order. Western writers, movies, and television have kept its legends circulating. Historians have recorded essential data and have frequently mentioned it in connection with events or famous people but there is little to be found in books pertaining to Arizona history concerning this stalwart structure of the frontier. Fortunately, a wealth of materials in articles and legal records has been preserved and it has been Mr. Jeffrey's purpose to assimilate the facts and publish a complete history from the enactment in the legislature to the closing of the Arizona Territorial Prison. As the status of this institution has been elevated to that of a State Park, the authentic story needs to be available to the public and therefore, the Yuma County Historical Society, Inc., is proud to sponsor *Adobe and Iron, The Story of the Arizona Territorial Prison* by John Mason Jeffrey.

YUMA COUNTY HISTORICAL SOCIETY, INC.
By Ruth E. Conner
Chairman, Publications Committee

CONTENTS

Frame of reference for proper evaluation.—Product of frontier.—
Typical Arizona construction.—Utilized new discoveries.—Present
ruins not typical.—Tough maximum security prison.—Location.—
Prison Hill conditionally deeded by Yuma.—Colorado River boundary
to prison area.—Indians paid to return escapees.—Need for prison.—
"Hard" men, violent times.—Isolation and lawlessness.—Effective
peace officers.—Inadequate jails.—Prison first public building of Territory.—Prison keystone of local economy.

Story of location.—Redondo: Father of the penitentiary.—First Prison
Commissioners.—A. L. Grow wins $150.00 for best plans.—Corner-
stone laid July 1, 1876.—Fifteen prisoners first guests.—Facility
eventually crowded.—Electricity in 1885.—New construction.—
Lowell Battery.—"Sallyport."—Engineering and construction of walls.
—Guard stations.—Library.—Snake Den.— Sewer system, cockroaches and bedbugs.—Fire in the laundry.—14,000 gallon auxiliary
tank.—Confinement problems.—Cell blocks.—Growing pains.—
Contagious ward.—New Yard.—Prison value at $175,000.00—De-
nied additional land for growth.—Drainage improvement.—Prison
filled real need.—Doomed for lack of expansion room.

Sixteen superintendents.—Appointed by the Territorial Governors.—
First Territory prisoners held in Yuma County jail.—Madora Ingalls
beloved of prisoners.—Two terms each for Ingalls and Gates.—Johnny
Behan from Tombstone.—Rynning, former Captain of Arizona Rangers, last superintendent.—Construction begun at Florence.—Yuma
prison abandoned September 15, 1909.—Guards.—B. F. Hartlee
the stalwart.—Prison officials.—"Country Club on the Colorado."—
Editorial criticism.—Prison Commissioners refuse to recognize succes-
sors.—Litigation.—Prison history generally uneventful.—Wages.—
Athletic programs.—Card gaming.—Prison Band.—Yuma church
choir.—School.—Limited facilities, but mission performed.

PREFACE

ARIZONA has long awaited an authentic history of its famous Territorial Prison. This work by John Mason Jeffrey establishes beyond all reasonable doubt that fact is more fascinating than fiction and truth more captivating than much nonsense that has been written about the pioneer institution.

From the time it was first occupied by a group of fifteen felons in 1876 until its abandonment thirty-four years later, the Territorial Prison attracted unusual attention. It was prominently located adjacent to the main transcontinental line of the Southern Pacific Railroad during a period of mass migration by rail. The austere appearance of the adobe walls, the ominous guards watching over sullen prisoners, and the sterile landscape and searing brightness of Arizona's sun gave it an air of mystery in a period when Arizona significantly was a last frontier in Western expansion.

But life behind the forbidding walls was not as dismal as might have been imagined. To the muster of Indian, Mexican, Chinese, Negro, and Anglo-American prisoners it was not necessarily a final destination without hope. Only a handful of prisoners languished there into old age. It was not a place of execution, although death through disease did hurdle the walls. Some daring men managed to escape to fitful freedom, while most of its prisoners earned shortened terms as compensation for their useful labor and good behavior. A few women—sordid frontier characters—added to the prison's drama. Whether innocent men were confined there was an argumentative point in the decade of the 1880s

when Mormon polygamists were being arrested and imprisoned on charges of cohabitation.

Mr. Jeffrey has studied and written the history of the prison with experienced mastery of a subject which developed
indirectly from his training as an attorney. It is an honest and
a true although not exhaustive history of an unfortunate but
real part of pioneer life.

The Arizona State Parks Board, in opening the prison to
public visitation and maintaining a museum on the historic
grounds, has recognized the great and growing interest of
Americans in the institutions that helped win the West to
civilization. The Territorial Prison was one of those agencies
of social stabilization. It may be seen and its history may be
studied with confidence that the representations made are as
honest as scholarly research can reveal.

BERT M. FIREMAN
Arizona Historical Foundation

Sources of illustrations are indicated by the following abbreviations:
(APHS) Arizona Pioneer Historical Society, (SWM) Southwest Museum, (YCHS) Yuma County Historical Society, and (YTPM) Yuma
Territorial Prison Museum. Other illustrations have been provided by
the author unless otherwise identified.

FOREWORD

Four years ago my wife Helen and I visited the Yuma Territorial Prison for the first time. Remaining long enough to make a few sketches, I developed an interest that probably would not have attended a shorter stay. When I left I determined to search back through the pages of time, and find the real story behind the ruins.

Our search was started off in the right direction by my friend and fellow Westerner, Dr. Ray Brandes. It lead us to the Archives in Phoenix, the State Prison at Florence, and libraries in Tucson, Los Angeles, San Diego, and elsewhere. Basic source material came on microfilm from the National Archives, the Arizona Pioneers' Historical Society, the Yuma City and County Library, and from local libraries.

Arizona newspapers from 1895 to 1909 were perused both by careful handling of the browning, disintegrated pages, and by microfilm. All material was copied as found, by longhand, on-the-spot type copying, dictated into a recorder, or by direct photocopy.

We read, and added to our files, every article from those magazines of that period to the present.

Frankly, when I started I expected to find quantities of horror stories. I thought my research would reveal a horrid Devil's Island in our own backyard. This was the concept played up by screen, TV, and many writers.

So, if I seem to be on the defensive in this book, please understand that I was fighting, from first to last, my own mis-begotten prejudices. If I found humanity, it was not because I didn't look for cruelty and shock.

It seems to me that the significance of the story is all the

deeper and more impressive because generally speaking there was order, fair dealing, and compassion. There were breaks and near riots, and prisoners trying to escape were shot, but the time taken by all these incidents put together wouldn't take seven 24-hour days,—not much considering 34 years of operation.

To help understand the phenomenon of the Arizona Territorial Prison we should keep in mind that the prison was really a community activity. The gates were open to the townspeople who came and went, selling merchandise and buying from the Bazaar, and visiting prisoners and guards. It was an operation in an amphitheater, as open to the public scrutiny as fish in a bowl. For any substantial scandal to have developed under such circumstances would have been an indictment of the whole town, if not the territory.

My thanks to Mr. William H. Haught, Park Ranger 2, Yuma; Miss Margaret Sparks of the Arizona Pioneers' Historical Society, Tucson; Mrs. Marguerite B. Cooley, Director, Arizona State Library and Archives, Phoenix; Superintendent Frank A. Eyman, Arizona State Prison, Florence; Mrs. Charlotte Tufts and Miss Joan West, Munk Library, Southwest Museum, Los Angeles; my good friends of the Yuma County Historical Society; and especially to Mr. Bert Fireman, Executive Vice President of the Arizona Historical Foundation, Tempe, who has advised me extensively and who has edited most of this book.

JOHN MASON JEFFREY

La Jolla, California

Following page: Sketch by Carl Eytel, of "A street in Yuma." (SWM)

ADOBE AND IRON

Prison as seen from Ft. Yuma on the California side of the Colorado River, showing west wall and Colorado River in quiet stage. (YTPM)

Cell blocks. Note foundations of demolished buildings. (Yuma Chamber of Commerce)

Following page: Sketch by Carl Eytel, of "Yuma Courthouse." The photograph appears on page 16. (SWM)

CHAPTER I
ERA AND AREA

HE Arizona Territorial Prison has been described with savage adjectives—grim, dreary, hellish, forlorn, forsaken, miserable—and even worse.

Stepping from his refrigerated automobile, after resting in an air-conditioned motel, today's visitor might unhesitatingly agree.

While indictments of such character were both common and substantially true during years of the prison's operation, 1876 to 1909, living conditions within its walls fairly represented the Arizona comforts and discomforts of the frontier of that period.

The prison and its operation can only be evaluated and appreciated when reviewed in a proper frame of reference. The visitor should attempt to understand that it was a product of the frontier soon after the Civil War and during a time of increasing outlawry in the Far West. In this light, its horror begins to fade and good points emerge.

Recognizing that homes and public buildings of the Southwest of that era were similarly, although often less substantially built, utilizing whatever material and labor were at hand, the prison further blends into its natural back-

Confluence of Colorado River and Gila River above the Narrows. The Main Guard Station rises above the horizon, just behind the Guards' Quarters. (YTPM)

This photograph, which was dated April, 1903, depicts the Colorado River in flood, with steamer and barge tied up in front of the U.S. Customs House. (Mr. and Mrs. Gilbert Sykes, Tucson)

14

ground. It was not an anachronism or a hellish place, but a desert and pioneer institution.

Hard as it might be to accept in this age, in some respects the prison was more comfortable than most homes in Yuma and the surrounding territory at the same time. In some ways it was so advanced that it has been credited with utilizing new discoveries and developments, such as electricity, forced ventilation, and sanitation.

Another point to help the visitor orient himself: the abrasive rock walls, so shockingly raw and primitive, were for the most part decently plastered and whitewashed or painted when the Territorial Prison was in use. It then presented a finished appearance, quite different from the stark impression that its ruins now leave. The place was busy with the activity, industry, and traffic of guards, prisoners and visitors providing a crowded picture.

This carefully accurate concept adds to the fascination of the Old Pen, its convicts, and its administration. The facts of the prison's existence were exciting and glamorous enough, without resorting to fiction or fabrication. There is some danger that one might err in the other direction, and imagine that it was a charming resort. No guard and no convict ever forgot that this was a maximum security prison. Here murderers and other callous criminals sweated out their sentences with the restiveness common to all confined creatures.

The editor of the *Arizona Republican*, of Phoenix, with pardonable enthusiasm in a Territory only recently freed from a quarter-century of Indian warfare, printed an article on the prison on August 24, 1890, which made the site appear inviting:

The Penitentiary is delightfully located on a hill overlooking the town and at a considerable elevation above it. To the north and east the Colorado leaves the base of the hill on which the Prison is located, and to the southeast the Gila flows into the

The town of Yuma in the early days of the Prison, seen on Prison Hill in the background. Guard Towers can be seen on the southwest and southeast corners of the wall, and the Main Guard Tower to their left. (YTPM)

Yuma County Courthouse, in Yuma, at the time of the Territorial Prison. (YTPM)

mighty river, forming a junction just beyond the Prison grounds. The location is most picturesque and attractive . . . On the opposite bluff in California, stands old Fort Yuma, now occupied as an Indian school under the direction of the Interior Department . . . To the south and east is the Valley of the Gila, as yet partially barren and practically uninhabited, but pregnant with the promises of an early awakening and destined to become one of the richest and most productive valleys of the Territory. To the south and southwest is the valley of the Colorado . . . In the sweep of the eye Pilot Knob arrests attention and marks the point where Mexico, California, Arizona intersect . . .

The picture is a pleasing and a satisfying one, but it also has a practical side. It is just such a place as a man trained in penology would select for a prison. Hemmed in by rivers and open valleys, escape is almost impossible . . . The drainage is perfect and the surroundings healthful, the elevation catches refreshing and invigorating breezes. The temperature is never very high, and the nights are nearly always cool and pleasant.

Anybody who has studied meteorological records or who has ever seen a television weather report will scoff at the writer's comment on the absence of high temperature in Yuma. He was badly mistaken; Yuma always has been one of the warmest cities in the nation.

The 8.38 acre hill on which the penitentiary was "delightfully" located had been deeded by the Town of Yuma to the Territory for penitentiary uses. The Colorado River then was navigable, making Yuma an important river port for steamboats traveling from the head of the Gulf of California northward into Arizona and Nevada. In its geological history the Colorado has cut its bed through a granite schist and caliche mesa, on which the prison is located. Its channel narrows to a few hundred feet separating the penitentiary on the south from old Fort Yuma on the north portion of the mesa. Rivermen called this channel The Narrows. The great volume of water forced through this funnel created

currents and hazards that would test the best swimmer, and
so inhibited the escape of convicts almost as much as did the
deserts beyond.

Mexico, but not always safety, lay a few miles to the
south. The savage desert in all directions created almost in-
superable problems for the man on foot, and was not lightly
to be challenged by the man on horseback.

The neighboring Quechan Indians, not yet a full generation from total savagery, crossed and recrossed this primitive
land with almost the same ease and freedom as the clouds in
the wide skies, and did so gladly to earn rewards of return-
ing escaped prisoners. Repressed to the point of rebellion by
the white man's laws, here was an area where their training
and instincts could be profitable. Escapees were fair game,
and the $50.00 reward was a prize equal to endless days of
menial toil. Some convicts were killed by the Indians: the
surprising thing is how many were returned to the prison
alive. The reward was the same. The advantage was that
the living prisoner didn't have to be carried.

Today penitentiaries are taken for granted. Every state
has one or two; some states have several. But in the new
Territory of Arizona, parted during Civil War years in
1863 from New Mexico Territory, the need for a maximum
security prison grew much more rapidly than its population.

A combination of geography, geology, climate, and circumstances created a frontier that irresistibly attracted that
rugged type of man who marches and fights and sometimes
vandalizes in the vanguard of civilization; a combination
that just as irresistibly resulted in a brazen lawlessness that
had to be dealt with by the Territory.

The Civil War left broken families, men, and States, and
contributed its part in supplying the men of purpose, and
the drifters, too, who sought their own particular pot of gold
in the "out beyond."

They came from everywhere in the United States and in

the world, and they all had two things in common: they were men of action, and they were men of exceptional courage. Inevitably this category must include in such an assortment of men of violence and men who had not done well or had not fitted in with society elsewhere. The half-humorous disparaging comment then in common usage in referring to an absent individual, as "G.T.T.," meaning "Gone to Texas," could have been applied to many of them. Usually the term implied an obligation unfulfilled, or a headlong dash on a lathered and heaving horse just ahead of a hard riding, but late starting, sheriff.

These early citizens were hard-working, hard-living, and just plain "hard," men. One and all stood ready, and had to stand ready, to defend self and property from violence or attack, recognizing that on this frontier it could not always be avoided. Until the 1890s the Indians were a constant, if somewhat of a sporadic, threat. Small parties of travelers were always fair game, as were the ranchers and the miners who dug in any distance from the settlements. These Indians fought a guerrilla type warfare, striking savagely and moving on, killing, and burning homesteads. Then they rode hard to the vastness of their mountain or desert retreats, or to sanctuary across the border to Mexico.

These Indians lacked the organization of their white antagonists, or the history of the Territory of Arizona would have been considerably more scarred and bloodstained than it is. Geronimo, Massai, and Victorio were not subdued until the last twenty years of the century, and within the memory of the last generation. In the half century prior to 1900, Arizona was a long, long way from the rest of the world.

It was this isolation which contributed in part to the lawlessness that was rampant in Arizona from the time of the Civil War. There were laws, but enforcement and punishment were twin problems. County sheriffs and Federal mar-

Panorama of Prison and Yuma from California side of the Colorado River, looking south. (APHS)

shals did not always cooperate with each other, or with the City marshals, to keep the peace. One of the more notorious examples of this lack of cooperation was the situation in Tombstone. Here the sheriff and marshal were not only enemies; they worked at cross purposes. The evidence is being sifted even now to judge the extent that the Tombstone sheriff and his gang were involved in the crimes they were sworn to suppress.

It is a fact that for years gangs killed, robbed, and rustled cattle without real interference.

For the most part, Arizona peace officers were able men with an almost incredible dedication and courage. They brought in their man one way or another, either alive and handcuffed, or head down across his saddle.

Those that were brought in alive then constituted a problem. Jails in the Territory were few and far between, and were wholly inadequate for anything but temporary deten-

tion. More than one jail was a mere hole in the ground, guarded by a deputy with a rifle. Prisoners escaped, and they escaped continually.

The good people of Arizona were trying to work their way out of the frontier practice of shooting or hanging its rustlers and thieves, and it was not much of an endorsement for the system of law enforcement if the criminal were to escape after having been duly convicted. The concept of a penitentiary was not new, even to the citizens of Arizona. At least it was not very new. Less than 100 years previously the first penitentiary had been built in Philadelphia, establishing a type that was to be patterned after by the prisons of Europe. Shortly after the Philadelphia Prison there was built in Auburn, New York, a different type of prison, which became the prototype for the penitentiaries of America. Almost every State had one or more. New Mexico, from which the Territory of Arizona had been so recently carved, was recognizing the need for a penitentiary, and started to build at Santa Fe about the same time as the Territory of Arizona did.

The Arizona Territorial Prison was one of the first major projects of the Territory. There were less than 50,000 people in the whole Territory—white, Mexican, or Indian— and money was hard to come by. This experiment did much to show Arizonians what could be done, and was a most important first step in the development of State government.

Yuma had only a few hundred population for many years during the life of the penitentiary. The institution sustained the town's business life while it dominated the geographic scene. Almost everyone was affected in some way by the penitentiary on Prison Hill. The guards and their families lived in town. Merchants and the services of craftsmen and others were always required to fill the prison's needs. It was the keystone of the local economy for many years, as well as a place of punishment and for some a tourist attraction. This

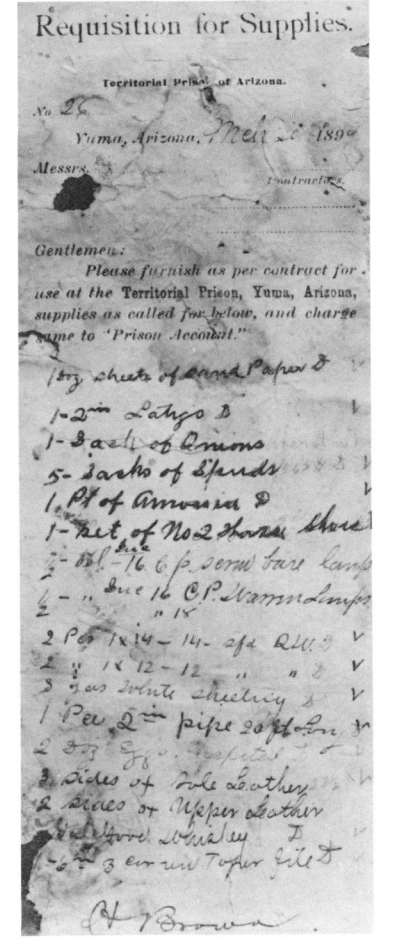

Painting of Grandville H. Oury, of Phoenix, Territory legislator who introduced the bill approving Prison Bond issue. (YTPM)

1896 photograph of Requisition for Supplies signed by Superintendent Brown. Deterioration of the paper keeps us from knowing how much "Good whiskey" was requisitioned along with the sand paper, latigo, onions, spuds, etc. (YTPM)

last role is retained, for in the ruins of the Arizona Territorial Prison the visitor may in a few minutes sense once more the trials and problems of the pioneer maldoer.

CHAPTER II

CONSTRUCTION AND DEVELOPMENT

NCE the need of a prison was established, the question of its location became important to the various towns and cities of the Territory. The Fifth Legislative Assembly in 1868 decided that the prison should be located at or near Phoenix. Fortunately for Yuma no action was taken on this bill, although it was passed.

Granville H. Oury of Phoenix introduced a bill in 1875 to the Eighth Territorial Legislature, approving a bond issue for construction of the prison previously authorized in 1869. Jose Maria Redondo (who was to become known as the father of the penitentiary) was an owner of a large part of Yuma County and Southern Arizona. He and Representative R. B. Kelly of Yuma County with political and parliamentry acumen and skill substituted "Yuma" for "Phoenix" in the Legislative Assembly. With this drastic change the bill passed, and the prison was Yuma's!

Redondo saw to it that there was no further delay. Bonds were issued, marketed, and sold to San Francisco financier A. Luther for $21,265.25. Currency fluctuations caused further attrition, and only about $19,000.00 in gold was actually realized by the Territory.

When Governor Anson P. K. Safford signed the bill into law, he appointed as the first Prison Commissioners prominent Yuma citizens, David Neahr and Jose Marie Redondo, and William H. Hardy of Hardyville. Captain Hardy, concerned that the distance from Yuma would prevent his attending meetings and occupied with his own affairs, did not accept the appointment, whereupon Governor Safford appointed Captain Isaac Polhamus, Jr., also of Yuma. Captain

23

Abe Frank. One of the early Prison
Commissioners. (YTPM)

David Neahr, one of the first three
Prison Commissioners. (YTPM)

Polhamus, a Colorado River pilot, was considered to be an
excellent choice. Only two of the three commissioners could
be from the same political party.

Interestingly enough, the plans for the Prison were those
submitted by a Yuma citizen, Mr. A. L. Grow. Instead of
commissioning or ordering plans, the new Board of Territorial Prison Commissioners shrewdly offered a prize of
$150.00 for the plans they would select. By adapting to the
locale, Mr. Grow won out over the more sophisticated plans
of San Francisco architects.

After languishing briefly, construction work accelerated,
and by February 1876 the excavation in the rocky hill for
the foundation of the building was proceeding steadily. The
engine for pumping water to the reservoir was in place, and
piping was being laid.

Prison Commissioner David Neahr, an accomplished
and thorough engineer, served as a general director of the
work. It was Mr. Neahr who ordered materials, tools and
equipment. These came from San Francisco via the Pacific

Ocean, the Gulf of California, and the Colorado River to the landing at Yuma. Engine, derrick, piping, tools, and implements, together with all the iron necessary, were acquired in this manner, and were paid for from the original appropriation of $25,000.00.

The prison was the first public building of note constructed in the Territory, and its construction as well as its operation was always distinguished by the most rigid economy.

On April 28th, 1876, about a year after Redondo's coup in the Legislature, the cornerstone was laid. Mayor A. J. Finley officiated at a simple ceremony attended by a few of the Yuma citizenry invited by the contractor L. A. Smith.

The *Arizona Sentinel* covered the occasion, and reported the collection of articles placed under the cornerstone as not being "very large, but sufficient to show the people who may inhabit this planet away down in the dim future, what kind of people erected this building . . . one copy of the *Arizona Sentinel*, of April 15th, 1876, and some pieces of United States silver coin."

The newspaper account continued, "The party then repaired to a shade nearby, where Mr. L. A. Smith had provided an ample supply of excellent refreshments to which full justice was done."

Thus refreshed, His Honor, Mayor of Yuma, one (which one wasn't reported) of the Penitentiary Commissioners, C. H. Brinley, Esq., Wm. J. Berry, and others, made appropriate remarks.

The report concluded without climax: "The party dispersed, and the workmen resumed their labor on the walls."

The fifteen prisoners who were led up Prison Hill July 1st, 1876, were no strangers to their new, permanent quarters. They had helped to construct them. There were two stone cells and an adobe building containing two prison rooms, a kitchen, a dining room, a hall room for Guards,

S.S. Cochran and barge tied to bank, March, 1905, in front of the U.S. Customs House. The Colorado River is again in flood. (Mr. and Mrs. Gilbert Sykes, Tucson)

Another view of Prison from California side showing caliche. (YCHS)

and Superintendent's quarters. The water reservoir had been completed with pump, boiler, and engine. It is of mild interest to us today that considerable emphasis was laid upon the existence of a "well equipped blacksmith shop." Reports of that day varied as to the number of prisoners that could be accommodated, the *Arizona Sentinel* of July 22nd, 1876, correcting a previous report by a statement that the Prison was capable of holding safely 32 prisoners. The buildings were enclosed by a wooden stockade which served until the great wall could be built.

As early as February 5, 1876, the *Arizona Sentinel* called upon the Yuma delegate to Congress to make every effort to have at least another $50,000.00 appropriated to finish the functioning but only partially completed penitentiary. $30,000.00 not $50,000.00 was authorized in 1879 by the Legislature, some earmarked for more cells and, importantly and consistent with the concepts of reformation and inmate improvement that were gaining acceptance in the nation's penal institutions, a substantial part of the appropriation was allocated to shops where the convicts could both be employed and acquire skills that might benefit them when they eventually reached the "outside."

Building continued. Cell blocks were added, and additional cells were blasted and chiseled out of the rocky hill.

Except for a flower garden there were few frills and little emphasis on decoration at the Prison. Two tests were applied to all proposed expenditures: Will they be functional? Are they necessary?

Every building and improvement on Prison Hill met these tests.

In time the top of Prison Hill became crowded inside as well as outside the walls. Stables, offices, and superintendent's residence were constructed outside of the front gate overlooking the Colorado River, in easy view of Fort Yuma on the California side.

Ex-Riverboat Captain F. S. Ingalls was one of the outstanding Superintendents of the Prison. (YTPM)

Prison Yard from a point near the Women's Yard. Note assortment of prison clothing. (APHS)

Superintendent Ingalls in 1885 had constructed a building 120 feet by 40 feet to accommodate the engine room, blacksmith, carpenter, shoe, and tailor shops. This building was enlarged in later years, and in 1895, the bakery and bath house were moved to this building by order of Superintendent Nugent.

One of the early important buildings contained the kitchen, bakery and the bathing room.

For nine years the prison depended upon coal oil and candles for its lighting. In 1885 electricity was provided by one of the first generators in the West. Three 1,500 candle-power lamps were powered by the first equipment. Ten years later a second generator was installed capable of providing power for Yuma. The economy-minded Commissioners made an agreement with the Yuma Light and Power Company to furnish electric power for the city after nine o'clock at night, in consideration for a continual supply of water pumped by the Power Company into the prison reservoir.

Hard use and developments in the production of electric power soon caused this equipment to become obsolete and of diminishing serviceability.

After the turn of the century Superintendent Griffith recommended that upon a completion of the New Yard a duplicate electric light plant be purchased and installed with all the machinery and workshop in the New Yard, at a cost of $50,000.00. A wall would separate the plant from the prisoners, and possible damage to the machinery in a break attempt would be avoided. Importantly, the location would release the necessary space for the construction of a new cell house.

Shops, dining room, photo gallery, and guard stations were added, and commanding the entire area was the Main Guard Station on top of the reservoir. The Main Guard Station and water reservoir under it have been preserved. Before it was torn down the wall at one point approached a point ten or fifteen feet from the Guard Tower. A catwalk connected the two, over which the rifle-carrying guards passed.

For many years a Lowell Battery, an improved design of Gatling Gun, was based on the floor of the Main Guard Station, where its formidable muzzles could be directed to any part of the prison yard.

Guard Tower over reservoir. Main entrance is just beyond the Gate-house. (YTPM)

Guard in Guard Tower with famous Lowell Battery. Highly maneuverable, this type of gatling gun was feared by the prisoners. (YTPM)

Only one gate was originally provided: the "Sallyport" or Main Gate. This huge archway, with its heavy strap-iron grilled door, remains. It is through this opening that visitors are admitted. As one enters one may visualize an unsmiling bemustached guard standing with his heavy 44-40 Winchester rifle cradled in the hollow of his arm; while browned, unshaven convicts, clad in a motley of prison stripes and colors, pause to stare, with eyes narrowed in appraisal and resentment at the newcomer. Clang! Don't worry. It's not locked.

As prison construction progressed, more and more of the hill was leveled, both to supply building space and building material.

The wooden stockade that was first constructed to contain the prisoners and some of the prison buildings over a period of time was replaced by a high adobe wall.

These walls were remarkably engineered. The foundation was constructed with solid rock obtained from the Prison Quarry, it being estimated that 51,000 cubic feet of rock and 60,000 pounds of lime were used in the construction of the foundation alone.

The height of the wall has been the subject of some dispute, since it has been variously reported by different sources. Many if not all of the discrepancies can be reconciled by the consideration of two factors. For one thing, the ground was not level over the whole top of Prison Hill, and to keep the top of the wall level, the height accordingly varied. A depression on the west side of the yard, for example, required construction to a height of 22 feet above the ground. Another factor was that the grade inside the walls varied from the grade outside. At the depression mentioned, where the height of the wall was 22 feet above the ground inside, the height of the wall on the outer side at this point was 39 feet. We may conclude that the average height of the wall was sixteen to eighteen feet.

East wall of Prison, with working party and drying adobes. (APHS)

Guard Hartley stands before the strap-iron gate of the Sallyport. The Gatehouse and the Sallyport have changed but little with the years, except for the superstructure to the concrete archway more recently added. (YTPM)

These walls were constructed of adobe block plastered smooth for appearance and protection against rain. Averaging eight feet wide at the base, the walls narrowed to five feet at the top, which was paved as a walkway for the patrolling guards. The prison yard was thus enclosed by walls on the west, north, and east sides, and the rocky hill itself on the south. From the vantage point of the top of the wall the guards, armed with Winchesters and pistols, commanded the situation. Every part of the yard could be seen from two or three walls. Here the vigilant guards could see everything, and were always in a position to be seen. Able to level their rifles on anyone in the compound, they were beyond the reach of any force or weapon that the prisoners might be able to make or secrete within the walls.

A double gateway was built into the middle of the north wall, which for many years was the only access to the prison yard. In 1903 another double gateway was constructed at the southeastern corner of the New Yard. It had an inside measurement of fourteen by thirty-two feet. Constructed of adobe, iron grating laid in the walls to a height of eight feet above the ground prevented prisoners from boring through.

The front gate remains, still hung with heavy iron work and double iron grated gates. The symmetrical design of the front in the Spanish style was a later addition, and was one of the few and not extravagant departures from the strictly functional.

The New Yard gateway had iron grating at the outer and inner entrances, as provided for the main gateway. In addition, the 1903 gateway supported a sixteen by thirty-two foot guard stand, designed to command both the inner and the outer gates. The stand was also used as a reloading room for ammunition and for other necessary armory work; the one large room being provided with lockers and work benches. The floor was of cement.

Also in 1903 two of the guard stations which had be-

View of the Territorial Prison from the south end of Prison Hill, looking northeast. The varying height of the wall may be noted. (YTPM)

Guard Station on the southeast corner, showing the windows and the
dreaded Lowell Battery. The Guard can be seen with his foot on the
window sill cradling his rifle over his knee. In the background on the
right is the Gila River. (YTPM)

come unserviceable were replaced by newer and larger stands, adding to the comfort of the guards, and giving them better command of both the inner and outer yards, and a smaller guard stand was constructed at the southwest corner of the yard.

On the cold winter nights when the winds howled down from the northern mountains across the cold desert, the guard stands provided welcome and needed protection for the guards who "had the duty" and patrolled the wall tops, leaning against the bitter cold and unchecked wind, high above the desert floor.

A deep cell was fitted as the library before it was housed in a separate building. A few shops hollowed out of the granite wall still remain, into which the insane were supposed to have been thrown for their protection as well as the protection of the rest of the prison population.

It is nearby that the notorious "Snake Den" is located. This dungeon was blasted out of caliche and is a room about fifteen feet square and twenty feet high, reached by a short corridor six or eight feet long. Formerly this corridor was blocked at both ends by iron doors, which not only kept the prisoners in, but served to keep light and air out. A small shaft from the ceiling to the top of the hill a few feet above, allowed forced ventilation and probably made this hole somewhat more bearable.

It was here that incorrigibles and refractory convicts were confined for one or several days on bread and water. It is gone now, but during the operation of the prison there was a strap-iron cage inside this square dungeon in which the unfortunate prisoners were locked. There was, of course, no running water and no sanitary facilities. Whether there was one convict or a dozen in "solitary," the furniture was probably never more than a canteen of water and perhaps a galvanized bucket.

Windowless Prison Library, excavated from north face of hill on south of prison grounds. (APHS)

Scene from the top of the hill into which the cells of the Women's Yard, the Library, and the Dungeon were chiseled. The hospital has not yet been built over the Cell Blocks on the right. Main Guard Tower, upper right center, aids orientation. Note ventilators at lower left. The long building along the north wall contains the shops. (YTPM)

There are at least two legends explaining how this dungeon received its name of "Snake Den." One is to the effect that a guard, or perhaps more than one, in a wicked exercise of malicious humor, dropped rattlesnakes and scorpions down through the ventilator shaft to torment the prisoners, as the latter sat or crawled around in the dark. One can imagine how the convicts speculated on this terror on hot summer nights, as they sweltered in their racks after lights out. It would not be surprising if veterans of that chamber of horrors, upon their return to the comparative comforts of their barred but airy cells, amplified their experiences, if indeed, they had not been convinced by their own terrors.

The other story is lighter, and probably enjoys greater support among those who are familiar with the history of the prison. One day a contingent of ladies from Yuma, interested then as now in the living conditions and well-being of the unwilling patrons of Yuma's major industry, visited the institution. The superintendent, in anticipation of the visit and fondly hoping to put on the best face possible, and the Dungeon at the time being unoccupied, ordered the ventilator shaft to be cleaned. As luck would have it, while the good ladies peered nervously into the rock hole, a family of scorpions was dislodged by the cleaning of the ventilator shaft, and they fell to the floor in the Dungeon.

The people of the Territory were not strangers to this type of varmint, but undoubtedly the environment did little to minimize the shock to the visitors. History does not record whether the ladies finished their tour. One thing is certain, if it happened in this way, the ladies lost little time in sharing the experience with their friends, and the experience did not suffer by the telling.

Not only was the old Dungeon called the "Snake Den," the present solitary confinement cell in the State Penitentiary in Florence is still called "Snakes." It is the only dungeon in the country so nicknamed.

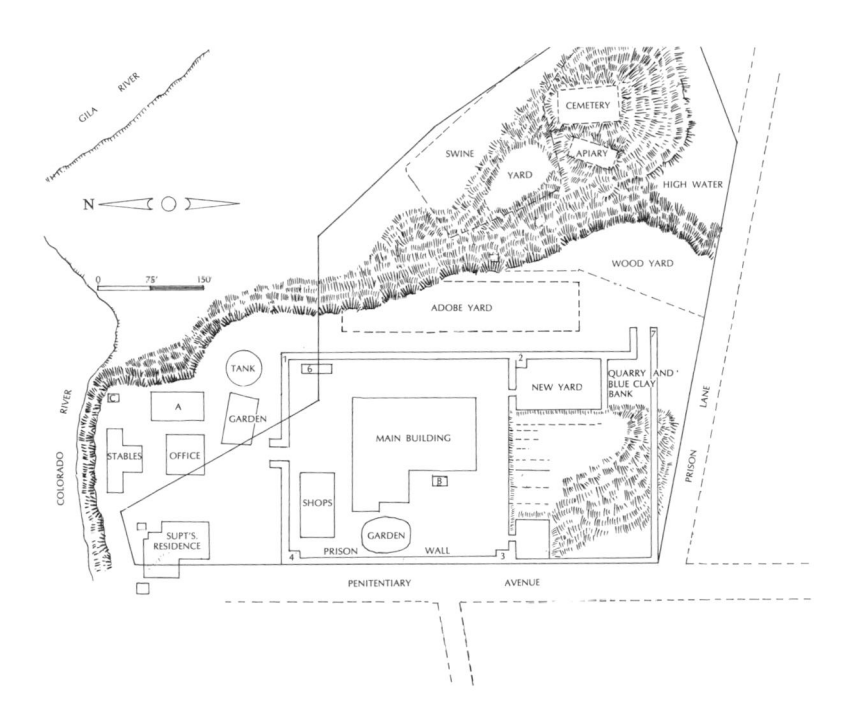

Yard at Arizona Territorial Prison about 1902.—A. Assistant Superintendent's Residence and Guards' Dormitory.—B. Photo gallery.—
C. Closets.— 1-7 Guards' Stations.

Not properly part of Prison Hill facility, but from time to time part of the prison operation, were the prison farm and wood camp. Closer to home, and on the eastern slope of the hill, were the swine yard, no longer identifiable, and the Cemetery. The latter is now fenced, and the wooden markers which once marked the last resting place of men who had enjoyed little rest during life have been lost and stolen except for two now in the Prison Museum.

The mass of humanity living in such a confined area created serious sanitary problems. We can guess by what was left unsaid or suggested, as much as by what was actually reported, that sewage disposal was a perennial trouble maker. Superintendent Behan installed a sewer system, and superintendents from then on complained about the sewer gases, as did their physicians, and it probably would not do the Old Pen an injustice to conclude that much of the time it was a smelly place.

The establishment was for an interminable period plagued by bedbugs and cockroaches. The central recollection of the beloved first curator, Mrs. Clarissa Winsor, was the large numbers of cockroaches that she observed on her visits there as a girl. This difficulty perhaps was never eliminated.

One infestation that was handled successfully, we are told, was that of bedbugs. For years these plagued the convicts. Control seemed impossible, in spite of various treatments.

At that time the bunk racks were made of lumber, and the bedbugs got down into the cracks. When Superintendent Griffith replaced these with iron bunk racks, he reported that this problem was met.

Another problem was never completely solved: that of water.

The water problem changed character, the emphasis moving from scarcity (due to pump failure) to impurity. In Territory days the Colorado River water was heavy with

This photograph, taken from the top of the Caliche hill at a point approximately over the "Snake Den," shows the railroad bridge in the background at Madison Street, repairs being made to the west wall under the Guard Tower, and the rear of the frame building (where the convict is leaning) which protected the west side of the double Cell Block from the sun and elements. The absence of this building now makes the Cell Block seem most uncomfortably exposed. (APHS)

Photograph of the Main Guard Station, taken after the Prison had closed and the wall had been torn down, showing the auxiliary water tank in the middle foreground. (YTPM)

silt, and had that rich reddish-brown color that gave the river its Spanish name "colorado."

This sediment phenomenon was not peculiar to the penitentiary. The townspeople in Yuma had the same trouble, and every home had one or more settling contraptions. Many townspeople used barrels in their backyards into which the river water was pumped and allowed to settle and attain some semblance of clarity.

Because these water systems were still in the experimental stage, and were considered such an improvement over previous techniques, few people were sufficiently disturbed by such problems to record them.

The inadequacy of the water supply was demonstrated graphically twenty years after the penitentiary first opened its door. On June 16th, 1896, at about 3:00 o'clock in the afternoon, flames caused by a defective flue in the laundry were discovered issuing from the roof. The laundry was in the new building recently erected, which contained the electric light plant, the shoe and tailor shops, and bath house. The guards immediately formed as large a fire-fighting detail as could work efficiently, there being no lack of manpower, but the building was entirely burned out. It was only by the most strenuous efforts of the staff and prisoners that the adjoining buildings were saved. The fire party was able to save nearly all the stockroom fixtures and shop tools, but the dynamo, switchboard, and all the electrical apparatus, were damaged beyond repair.

Reconstruction was begun at once, and when the new building had been completed with dynamo and fixtures in place, Superintendent Mike Nugent was able to record that the total cost was only $1,268.11, well within his original estimate.

Not to be caught again in the predicament of being unable to control fires, the superintendent purchased a handpower fire pump and 300 feet of three-inch hose, which

Convicts at leisure in Prison Yard dominated by Guard Tower. (APHS)

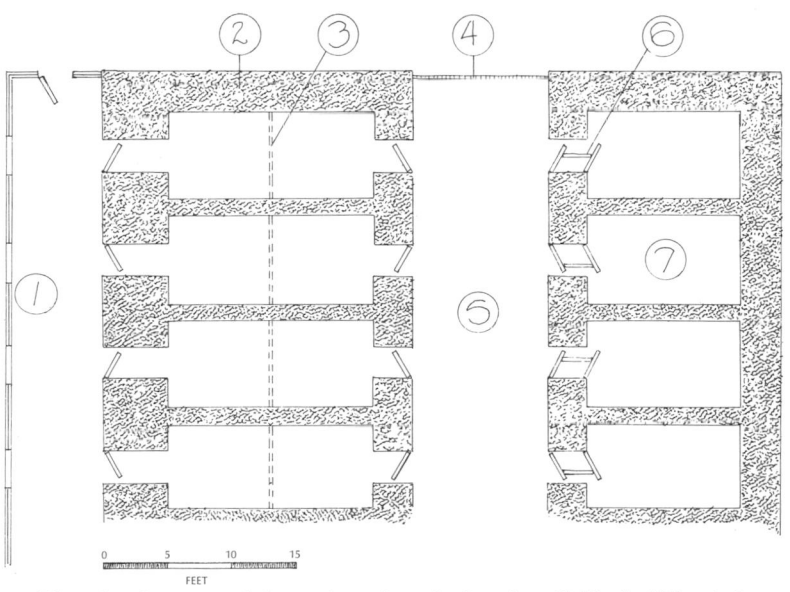

Plan showing ground floor of north end of main cell block (Hospital on the second floor).—1. Corridor to row of double cells (size and detail reconstructed).—2. Wall-granite and concrete.—3. Iron grill separating cells.—4. Iron grill.—5. Corridor.—6. Double doors-iron grill.—7. Single cells-long termers.

were kept within the prison enclosure. Thus progress followed experience at the Arizona Territorial Prison.

In 1904, 100 feet of new four-inch wrought-iron pipe replaced a troublesome main in the prison yard, and it is safe to assume that maintenance was a regular chore.

The water supply system was greatly improved by the construction of an auxiliary tank with a capacity of 14,000 gallons. This new tank was constructed of heavy galvanized iron, adjoining the main system, and was supported by a solid rock foundation eight feet high. It was enclosed with a framework, and a room twenty by thirty feet square was constructed on top, designed as Guards' Quarters.

Apparently the construction of the auxiliary tank did a great deal to meet the problem of muddy water. Superintendent Griffith had observed practically that the water was "almost unfit for drinking or cooking purposes, as well as causing unnecessary wear on the engine and boiler and lighting plant." Alternate use of the tanks permitted the mud to settle out of one tank as the other was being used.

The first and basic need of the prison was an adequate confinement area for the increasing numbers of prisoners. The program of adding cells never stopped until the prison was abandoned.

More cells were added to the first two until finally facilities were available, in a pinch, for over 400 inmates. Cells were hollowed out of the hill on the south side of the yard, first along the side facing the yard, and were used for shops, library, and solitary confinement. Then cells were hewn out of the rock mesa on the west side, for the Women's yard, facing a private yard 30 feet by 30 feet. Three of these cells can now be seen, driving up from the highway approaching Prison Hill. Women played a small but spectacular part in the history of the Arizona Territorial Prison, discussed more in another chapter.

When the Main Cell Block was constructed in 1895,

designed to hold 150 prisoners, the Prison Commissioners undoubtedly (but mistakenly) thought they had finally licked their space problem. The ruins of these cells still remain standing south of the Museum.

The Main Cell Block consisted of two parallel blocks of cells, running north and south. The cell block on the west side contained fourteen parallel, airy, double cells: long rooms running across the building and partitioned in the middle by a heavy iron grate. Both buildings were 132 feet long, whereas the east cell block (with single cells) was 18 feet wide, and the west cell block (with double cells) was 24 feet wide. The two cell blocks were separated by a distance of about ten feet. The walls were all approximately three feet thick, excepting the west wall of the west block, which was five feet thick. These widths obtained about three feet above ground level. The walls narrowed slightly as they increased in height.

The east, single-cell block held the long-term prisoners. These cells are much in the same condition they were in 1909 when abandoned. These had two metal barred doors, opened in unison, being held together by a cross bar. They provided an opening just large enough for a prisoner to go around one door and then the other.

The west block cells were for the short-term prisoners, and had only one door to a cell. Four double cells have been torn down now, and today this block is some 36 feet shorter than the other.

In 1904 Prison Physician J. A. Ketcherside echoed the perennial complaint to the effect that the only serious problem at the Prison was the lack of cell room. He stated,

Every cell in the Prison is now utilized to its full capacity, there being from four to six men in the small cells and eight to twelve in the larger ones, where for sanitary and for other reasons there should not be more than two occupants in each cell.

The Prison Commission and the superintendent continued their efforts to cope with the steady stream of new convicts.

During 1903 and 1904 the superintendent constructed five additional cells. Toolproof steel caging had been procured from the Champion Iron Company of Canton, Ohio. A plastered adobe building with galvanized roofing was built on the west side of the Main Cell House for the installation of these new cages. This building was 48 feet by 26 feet. The maximum security prisoners were kept here. This cell block is now gone.

Some relief was gained by allowing a number of the most trusted prisoners to sleep on cots outside the cells in the Yard.

Superintendent Griffith did not like the idea of having twelve men in the double and six men in the single cells. Without going into detail he observed,

For the proper observance of discipline, and to prevent the practice of pernicious habits, as a result of the overcrowded cells, each cell should not have more than two occupants.

He requested funds to purchase a 60 cell, double deck steel cage. He estimated the cost in Bessemer steel at $25,000.00, and if made of toolproof steel, at approximately $34,000.00. For the installation of this cage he recommended construction of a building 176 feet by 35 feet, adjoining the Main Prison Cell House on the east side. This was the ground then occupied by the electric light plant, laundry, shoe and tailor shop, bathroom and library, the building to be constructed to contain a library room in addition to the cage.

In constant use as punishment cells and for the isolation of prisoners afflicted with contagious and infectious diseases, were the cells in that portion of the hill forming the south wall of the Main Yard, the west wall of the New Yard, and the east wall of the Women's Yard.

45

Cells hammered into caliche hillside at south end of prison grounds in area then known as the "New Yard." Ventilators can be seen on the left, and the tall light-pole with electric light on north side of the hill. Note chair at extreme left, and the open doors to the cells. Except for the incorrigibles, prisoners were allowed out of their cells during the day. These cells with eastern exposure were probably cooler than those in the Women's Yard, on the west side. Note electric wires strung on the face of the wall over the doors. (APHS)

Same cells as shown in previous photograph. This picture illustrates the disrepair caused by erosion which almost completely changes the tone of the prison from one of plain efficiency to one of brooding horror. The leveling of the adobe walls has raised the level of the ground. (Mrs. Clarissa Winsor)

The last cells to be added were hewn out of the east side of the hill, on the side opposite from the Women's Yard, in the area described in the reports as the New Yard. These cells remain, and are notable for their particular barrenness and rawness, and for the fact that their floors are now several inches below the level of the outside yard. This phenomenon is perhaps the result not so much of blowing sand and dirt as the leveling of the adobe walls.

Originally the front of these cells was faced with adobe and plaster, and at that time no doubt presented a finished and acceptable appearance. Now the plaster is gone, the adobe is eroding, and the aspect is one of melancholy desolation.

The Main Cell Block, those two parallel concrete and granite structures, received a second story in 1901, which became a much needed and appreciated hospital. There the walls did not block whatever breezes might tend to make the hot summer nights more bearable, and the corridor thus covered permitted the accommodation of prisoners in this substantial area.

In Superintendent Griffith's Report of June, 1904, the value of the Prison improvements was estimated at $175,-000.00. This represented an increase of valuation of $25,-000.00 over the valuation set by his predecessor Superintendent Herbert Brown.

The superintendent reported with some annoyance that the City Council of Yuma had refused to lease the prison any more land, but what he recommended was that if further property could be secured, "I will recommend that the buildings thereon be demolished and new structures erected in keeping with the need and growth of the prison. The prison buildings are wholly unserviceable and should be replaced by modern offices."

In the years 1903 and 1904, work was done to install a drainage system for the yard, which during rainy weather

Northwest corner of wall and Superintendent's Home on right. A portion of "Rincon Alley" is visible between Prison Hill and railroad station. Railroad bridge formerly crossed the Colorado south of its present location, at Madison Street. (Clarence DeCorse, Yuma) (YCHS)

Front gate—"Sallyport," Gate House, and North Wall. Note garden, stacked tools, and light pole. The ubiquitous chair can be seen at the west edge of the garden. (APHS)

had been covered with water and mud. A complex of six-inch pipe was laid, and the yard was brought down to a proper grade and covered to a depth of six inches with crushed rock. This in turn was covered with a layer of blue dirt, "well stamped to make a smooth and solid surface." Decomposed granite brought from a granite bank about a mile away, and having a clayey nature, made a macadam-like top and final dressing.

Catch basins with grated tops were placed about the yard and the superintendent reported, "The drainage is now excellent, the water quickly passing off into the catch basins, leaving the yard in good condition at all times."

The outside yard between the Main Gateway and the office was completed during this period by being surfaced with blue dirt and decomposed granite.

It was in the matter of the physical plant that the Old Pen differed most from other prisons. Penitentiary construction everywhere else had followed conventional lines, much like the present State Penitentiary at Florence.

There was nothing "nice" about the Territorial Prison physical plant. Everything was functional and because of required economies usually short of being adequate.

Most of the cells were throwbacks to the caveman days and the accommodations as a prison were substandard.

In saying this we should not overlook two important facts: first, the facilities did a man's job in accomplishing its mission well for the Arizona Frontier of that period, and secondly, if comparisons are to be made with other penitentiaries, an overall comparison, not limited just to the physical plant, would have been favorable to the Old Pen. For that time and that place in history, the Old Pen was, we must admit, something of a marvel.

It grew like Topsy from its initial set of $150.00 plans, but in the long run it was not the failure of the facilities, but the lack of expansion room, that doomed the prison.

Fourth Superintendent, Thomas Gates, was one of the better known administrators. His instructions to the Guards to fire in the event of an attempted break, even though staff lives might be endangered, probably was responsible for aborting the break of 1887. (YTPM)

Portrait of Superintendent Thomas Gates painted by one of the prisoners. (YTPM)

Prison Physician J. A. Ketcherside. (YTPM)

Mrs. Madora Ingalls, wife of Superintendent F. S. Ingalls. Mrs. Ingalls worked tirelessly to improve the lot of the convicts. (YTPM)

CHAPTER III

ADMINISTRATION

NLY sixteen men held the job of superintendent (some prisons elsewhere used the term "warden") during the 34 years of operation of the Territorial Prison. They set the tone of that institution, and should be presented.

During the formative period of prison planning and construction the elected sheriff of Yuma County, William A. Wernniger, was appointed by the Territorial Governor as the first superintendent. He held that office as well as his local law enforcement job for several months. There was a very good practical reason for this. Prisoners were being sent to the prison at Yuma before it was finished. So the adobe Yuma County jail served as de facto prison until the structure on the hill was completed.

Wernniger's term began in 1875 and overlapped that of his successor, George M. Thurlow. The latter was appointed on January 22, 1876, and took office five months later on June 22. But as late as June 28—pending the final completion of the new prison—Wernniger still considered himself superintendent and signed a receipt for the delivery of three felons from Yavapai County. These prisoners were held in the Yuma County jail until July 1 when fifteen shackled men marched up the hill to more comfortable quarters than Wernniger had been able to provide them. Thurlow served five full years, resigning January 11, 1881.

T. V. Meeden was the third superintendent. His term was for two-and-a-half years and was relatively uneventful.

F. S. Ingalls replaced Meeden on June 12, 1883. A former river boat captain, he served for three years as one of the most distinguished and enlightened gentlemen to hold

that office. His wife Madora worked continuously for the betterment of conditions and for the education of the convicts, and was universally loved by them. Courageous and practical as well as warm hearted, Madora Ingalls once helped fire the Lowell Battery in a prison break. Captain Ingalls was one of two superintendents to serve two separate terms, an indication of his popularity and efficiency. His first term ended July 6, 1886.

Thomas Gates followed Ingalls' first term in 1886. His also was one of the stronger administrations. Another chapter describes how he helped quell the prison break in 1887.

The next superintendent was a man well known to Arizona at that time, a former Yavapai County legislator who served as sheriff of Cochise County in its most turbulent times. Colorful John H. Behan will be remembered by most as an adversary of Wyatt Earp and Doc Holliday in Tombstone. Dignity may not have been his forte and he had little talent for administration, but he was a frontiersman of great courage and coolness. During much of his three years as superintendent he was under a fierce barrage of newspaper editorials, some of which could have been a carry-over from his difficult role in Tombstone.

Captain Ingalls was returned for a second term on October 7, 1899, to restore the prestige and efficiency of the prison. When this had been done he stepped down on September 3, 1891, to attend to private business interests, making way for a man both controversial and effective, M. M. McInernay.

Superintendents were political appointees in a period when patronage and the spoils system were the way of public life. They were frequently subjected to political criticism. Although Superintendent McInernay clearly improved recording procedures and in 1892 submitted a biennial report to the governor of more than a hundred printed pages, the *Arizona Daily Star* of Tucson wrote that he ran the prison in

a "reckless and unsystematic manner," accusing him of ignoring business routines and allowing relaxation of discipline. This attack upon Mr. McInernay is not sustained by the record. During his term from September 3, 1891, to April 15, 1893, the penitentiary was improved by new construction, repairs, and refittings, such as:

The old system of water closets which, in addition to being inadequate to accommodate the number of prisoners, was also a menace to the health of the Prison, has been torn down and replaced with Parson's trough system of closets, which so far has given complete satisfaction.

McInernay further reported:

The guard stands have been put in good condition and enclosed in a framework of glass as a protection against the weather which, contrary to popular impression, is quite severe during the winter nights. The enclosed space does not in any way interfere with the Guard's observation of his surroundings, and renders his position a great deal more comfortable.

Former Superintendent McInernay, after he had left the penitentiary, was tried for the crime of embezzlement. He was acquitted, and the editorial comment was to the effect that he had been the victim of political enemies and that his acquittal was nothing more than simple justice.

William K. Meade's term as superintendent was curiously brief, and the reasons therefor were unreported. In less than three months he was replaced by ailing Thomas Gates, on July 13, 1893. We can speculate that the problem was one of health for part of Meade's short term the prison was under actual control of M. I. Shaw, acting superintendent.

Thomas Gates' second term began on April 15, 1893, and lasted until 1896.

Mike J. Nugent served the year from July 14, 1896, to July 31, 1897.

John W. Dorrington, a fiery Yuma newspaper editor,

Group of Prison Guards and Staff, with mascot. Juan Zavala, second from right in back row, is pictured on page 86 as a much younger man.

The "Queen of the Bandits," Pearl Hart, posing with pistols and rifle. (APHS)

Pearl Hart, sullen with bowl haircut and number. (APHS)

served only a month or so over a year, from July 31, 1897, to September 10, 1898.

At the turn of the century Herbert Brown was a strong successor who did much to increase the caliber of the prison. He served for almost four years, from September 10, 1898, to June 4, 1902.

The next superintendent, William M. Griffith, was a competent administrator. He served for two years from June 4, 1902, to October 3, 1904.

R. F. Daniels served less than a year, from October 3, 1904, to June 5, 1905.

Jerry Millay was well liked as a man, but the institution suffered under his administration as well as that of Daniels. In this decline there was a need for better control.

On January 4, 1907, the final territorial superintendent, Thomas Rynning, took over with a strong and effective hand. A former captain of the Arizona Rangers and an engineer, Rynning was soon to supervise construction of the new prison at Florence. Much of his administration Rynning spent there, supervising construction, making good use of the manpower of trustworthy convicts. Initially eighteen longtime prisoners were taken to Florence to work, and others were added until the work force amounted to about 140, leaving behind at Yuma the forty less reliable and the female convicts. On September 15, 1909, the last 40 inmates were marched to a waiting train to be taken to Florence, handcuffed and hitched in pairs to a long chain. Assistant Superintendent Wilder remained in charge at Yuma until its close on September 15, 1909. Rynning, unlike his predecessors, survived changes in the governor's office and still was superintendent when Arizona attained statehood in 1912.

Not a great deal of information is readily available about the guards. Some names remained on the payroll for year after year. While appointment as a prison guard was a common political reward at the time, the records indicate that

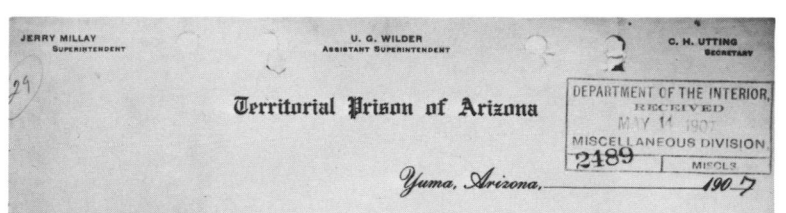

JERRY MILLAY
SUPERINTENDENT

U. G. WILDER
ASSISTANT SUPERINTENDENT

C. H. UTTING
SECRETARY

Territorial Prison of Arizona

DEPARTMENT OF THE INTERIOR,
RECEIVED
MAY 14 1907
MISCELLANEOUS DIVISION
2489   MISCLS.

Yuma, Arizona, _____ 190_7_

To the Honorable Board of Control :-

I respectfully submit to you my report of the management of
the Territorial Prison of Arizona,for the biennial period ending
June 30,1906. Accompanying this report are statements and tables,
from the heads of the various departments,showing in detail the operations for two years.

The population of the prison July 1,1904,was 294. At the
close of that fiscal year,329; an increase of 35. At the close of
the fiscal year,June 30,1906,360; an increase during that year of
31,and an increase of 66 during the two years covered by this report.

This increase of the criminal population of the Territory,in
such a short period,causes us to squarely face one of two alternatives: either a new prison,fitted up with modern improvements,
with more room and better accommodations,or an extension of the
grounds here,with the addition of more cell-room ,and other much
needed improvements.

There is now,in actual use,in good condition,cell room to
accommodate 224 persons; 204 in the regular prison cell rooms,and
a place where 20 could be accommodated in the new incorrigible
ward,should so many inmates need to be disciplined. Up to date,
not over ten have been confined therein since its completion.

In order to accommodate 204 in the main cell room,six men
must be crowded into each cell. While this condition of things
may not cause actual suffering during the winter, it is almost
unbearable during the summer months. Although a blower runs con-
stantly from 5 P.M.,when the men are locked in the cells,until
5:45 in the morning,when they are released,it is nevertheless a
condition which should not be permitted. The men are not sent here
to be punished,but are punished by being sent here and being deprived of their liberty. The balance of the prisoners are located
in various places to sleep; some in the corridor,some in excava-
tions under ground,and some in the yard,known as the "chronic yard,"
where there are 12 cells dug in the bank,and fitted with iron doors.
These are makeshifts that suffice to sleep the better and safer
class of prisoners,but in no case are they absolutely safe,thus
necessitating great care in selection,and extra guards for absolute safety.

At least as much more cell-room as we have now is,or soon
will be,an absolute necessity,and the only place I can discover
where it can be placed is on top of the other cell house. To do
this the hospital which is almost new,would have to be moved.

The dining room is much overcrowded,and must be enlarged,and
possibly the hospital might be placed over the dining room.

First page of the Biennial Report of Superintendent Jerry Millay, for
the period ending June 30, 1906. (National Archives and Records
Service)

many men made careers of such employment, successfully avoiding the political mortality of superintendents.

B. F. Hartlee was by far the most outstanding and best known guard at Yuma, particularly noted for his courage, coolness, and unerring rifle fire in the October 27, 1887 break. On several occasions he demonstrated such capabilities. He was at times assistant superintendent, and if he had desired the post might have been superintendent. He held his job on the prison staff during Republican administrations although he was openly a Democrat. When the Republican *Tucson Citizen* begrudged him his $85.00 per month salary because he was one of the "out" party, partisans of both parties rallied to his support. The *Arizona Sentinel* somewhat extravagantly claimed that Hartlee had saved the city of Yuma from being sacked by convicts in 1887. All realized he had saved the life of Superintendent Gates. Hartlee had no political aspirations, however. He was contented to serve as a guard. It was October, 1892, before his salary was raised to $100.00 per month.

The superintendent was chief executive officer of the prison, and was supported by an assistant superintendent (sometimes called by the title "Turnkey"), yard captain in charge of guards, captain of the night watch, a secretary and a storekeeper.

For the first fifteen years of the prison a doctor was called from Yuma to treat the sick and injured, but eventually a full-time physician was authorized.

Until 1895 the Board of Prison Commissioners established the policies of the prison, the members being appointed by and responsible to the territorial governor. In 1895 the prison and the insane asylum (and later the Reform School) were put under the jurisdiction of one board, called the Board of Control. The superintendent answered to this board, whose three members were recruited from different parts of the Territory. Thus its personnel and eventu-

No.	Name	Crime Rec'd. Term	County Com. of Sent	G.T. Ex. of S.
1494	J. Devilla	Assault 6/18/99 10 yrs	Cochise June 17, 1899	42 mo. Dec.16/05
1495	R. Castro	Forgery "	" " "	17 " Jan.16/03
1496	A. Otero	Murder " Life	" " "	— At Death
1497	P. Acosta	" " "	" " "	—
1499	J. McKinley	Burglary 6/9/99 5 yrs	Yavapai " "	17 mo. Jan.16/03
1501	T. Plummer	Murder " 20 "	" " "	92 " Oct.16/11
1503	H. Wilber	" 6/25/99 15 "	Maricopa " 12, "	67 " Nov.11/08
1504	J. Gatlan	G.L. 6/27/99 10 "	Gila " 26, "	42 " Feb.5/08
1509	E. Barnes	Murder 7/12/99 Life	Yavapai July 10 "	— At Death
1510	H. Hutchinson	G.L. " 5 yrs	" " "	17 mo. Jan.30/03
1511	V. Lucero	Murder " Life	" June 26 "	— At Death
1525	J. Brown	Burg. 10/4/99 5 yrs	Maricopa Oct. 4	17 mo. May 4/03
1539	D. Rodriguez	Murder 10/13/99 Life	Graham " 16 "	— At Death
1543	J. Brown	" 10/23/99 20 yrs	Mohave " 21, "	92 mo. Feb.20/12
1549	L. Sandoval	Assault 10/4/99 7 "	Pima " 18, "	27 " July 13/04
1550	J. Lindale	Rape " 8 "	" " 19, "	33 " Feb.18/05
1554	Earl Hart	Robbery 11/18/99 5 "	Pinal Nov. 17 "	17 " June 16/03
1568	P. Brady	Grand Larceny 12/1/99 5 "	" " 29 "	17 " " 28/03
1579	E. Mata	Murder 12/18/99 Life	Apache " " "	— At Death

Copy of page from pocket Journal of J. M. Clark, a Prison Guard, showing numbers and other data pertaining to prisoners in confinement about the turn of the century. The original notebook is on display at the Prison Museum.

ally its policies were subject to political vagaries. The prison budget was fixed by the legislature.

It is from the reports of the prison physician and other staff members to the superintendent, reports of superintendents to the Board of Prison Commissioners and Board of Control, their reports to the governors, and the reports of governors to the territorial legislatures and to the Federal Department of the Interior that we are chiefly indebted for reliable information on the prison operations.

Critics sometimes called the prison "The Country Club on the Colorado." This suggested that inmates were there by choice, and that they were happier or better off in prison than

they had been elsewhere. The *Arizona Sentinel*, during a period of editorial hostility, described it as a place of "recreation and amusement" with reading, singing, and skylarking, where one and all had a "grand old time."

Undoubtedly there were periods of lax enforcement of prison rules. The atmosphere, discipline, and operation changed from superintendent to superintendent, and must have changed within administrations as personnel acquired experience and attitudes changed.

On April 29, 1890, the *Tucson Fronterizo* leveled an attack on the prison administration.

A gentleman that was here some days ago and was in Yuma for a day . . .

With what might appear as slight opportunity for observation, this gentleman charged that Mexican prisoners were treated with excessive severity,

making them suffer more cruelly than the exiles to Russian Siberia, giving them the hardest labor, less food and clothing than to others, and of the hardest punishments for any insignificant cause.

Specifically he charged that a Mexican prisoner had deposited $150.00 with the superintendent, and subsequently requesting credit for the same, was punished with forty days in the

dark cell . . . with bread and water (and) in consequence of that injustice is now in a lamentable condition of health, without letter writing privileges or communication with the outside.

The Yuma paper sprang to the defense of the prison, emphasizing its own "careful investigation of the matter." The tone was lofty.

The Editor of the *Fronterizo* has been imposed upon by his informant. The statement . . . is untrue and without foundation in every particular.

59

In the first place no prisoner has ever been put into the dark cell for a period of 40 days; . . . a report is made (and published quarterly) showing name and length of time in the 'dark cell.' . . . Once a week all of the prisoners are allowed to write letters to their friends. Upon inquiry it was found that no prisoner ever asked for a receipt for money he might have on deposit, and furthermore, all the Mexican convicts taken together have not got the sum of one hundred and fifty dollars.

Earlier that month a greater political storm had shaken the Board of Prison Commissioners. Republican Governor Lewis Wolfley had made two appointments to the board, William C. Davis and A. E. Cutter. Two incumbent commissioners, P. R. Frady and Thomas Hallack, were unwilling to surrender their positions.

The third member of the Board, W. B. Robbins of Cochise County, avoided direct involvement in the struggle.

Although his wide political experience should have taught him that in public life "those who live by the sword die by the sword," Johnny Behan also tried to hang on to his job as superintendent after his successor—Captain Frank Ingalls—had been named by the newly appointed commissioners. The political hassle had another aspect; the secretary of the board also held a paid position as the prison secretary. While the two commissioners and Behan challenged the governor, Secretary J. J. Stein declined to hand over his books and records to his successor, Judge C. H. Brinley of Yuma.

All the unseated appointees filed suit in U.S. District Court. Judge Hames H. Kibbey was then sitting in Yuma, but he adjourned the session, ruling that the matter should be heard on neutral ground in Phoenix. There the court ruled in favor of the new governor's appointments.

The prison commissioners came in for sharp criticism for entering into a contract to provide convict labor to a private irrigation company. The governor condemned the arrange-

ment charging that the prisoners were being exploited and ordering an action filed to cancel the contract. Unsuccessful in the trial court the Territory prevailed upon appeal, and the contract was voided.

In retrospect, the history of the Old Pen was remarkably uneventful. Considering that almost 34 years were involved, with no large scale riots, with less than a half dozen breaks (and these involving only a few prisoners), and little cause for scandal, the mild nature of most contemporary observations and the content of prison reports reveal a relatively simple, quiet prison operation, surprisingly unmarked by violence.

The superintendents were decently, although not lavishly, paid for their services and responsibility. Their monthly salaries were $250.00 for most of the 34 years. They took a salary cut about the turn of the century, and the reports of 1898-9 and those as late as 1904 reveal varying pay as low as $175.00 per month.

This was good pay, considering the value of the dollar and the absence of "deductions." Moreover, the superintendent was provided with an ample residence, well furnished in the mode of the area and the day, and the prison commissary furnished food for his table. There was always a surplus of manpower to meet the current needs for yard and house work, and the prison team and buggy took care of all local transportation. Official travel was of course paid by the Territory.

The wage of the assistant superintendents dropped sharply to $125.00 per month, just half of the salary of the superintendent.

Guards' wages varied, but for most of the prison operation the starting pay was $75.00 per month, with a high of $100.00 paid to those more senior or better oriented politically.

Yuma was a sleepy town in those days, and we can im-

Unidentified Guard. (APHS)   Unidentified Guard. (APHS)

Unidentified Guard. (APHS)   Guard Hartlee. (YTPM)

agine that Prison Hill was sleepy, too. Evidently there was understanding and even friendship between many of the guards and convicts. Prison working parties, repairing levees and roads, were so much a part of the background that they were hardly noticed by the townspeople.

The incorrigibles and the dangerous, and there was an ample supply of these, were dealt with firmly. Discipline, not psychology, was the keynote of their treatment. This worked. They were kept from society, and Arizona prospered.

Organized athletic programs for prisons had not become generally popular even by 1909, and there is no record of any such program at the prison. One old photograph shows a "human pyramid," with three prisoners standing in the prison yard holding two more in the air, who in turn held aloft a third. The caption indicated that these prisoners were exercising. We can imagine that the guards on the wall preferred exercises and games that would not get the prisoners so close to the top of the wall.

The prisoners did play cards, sometimes freely but usually surreptitiously, since gambling was forbidden. Quoits, simple games of Mexican origin, and other diversions helped the inmates while away some of the long, hot hours.

Toward the last years of the prison the Yuma Bandmaster formed a Prison Band, numbering some 40 members. There were no radios, television, or movies, and it is impossible to even guess at the enormous entertainment given the convicts by the Prison Band concerts. The band played only within the prison walls, and only on Sundays, but these were red letter days for the convicts. No matter how long the programs, they were always too short. Encore after encore was entreated by the highly appreciative, if unsophisticated, audience.

The prisoners were afforded another form of music, which also made them look forward eagerly to Sundays. On Sun-

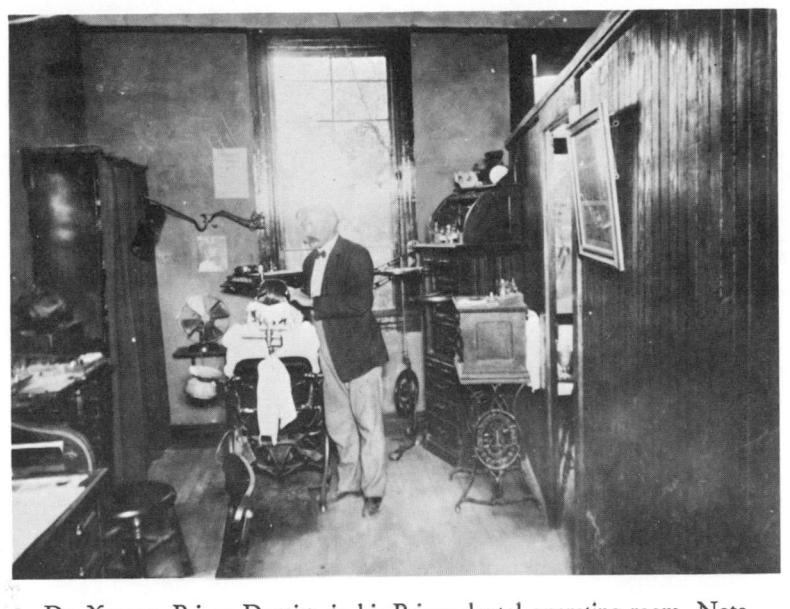

Dr. Yeman, Prison Dentist, in his Prison dental operating room. Note the roll top desk and cabinet. (YTPM)

day mornings a choir, composed of little girls and young women from one of the Yuma churches, came and sang hymns for the unfortunates on Prison Hill. Some Yuma ladies remember singing in this choir, and associate no fear or distaste with that experience.

A school of sorts was maintained from time to time, some-times taught by the more educated prisoners themselves. The English language was the most popular subject, but other languages were also taught. Many prisoners who could not

Letter of high tribute to Mrs. Madora Ingalls, beloved wife of the then Superintendent, signed by the prisoners. Note that there were 2 Chinese. It would appear that at least 3 of the prisoners could not write, but made their x, and had their names added by the beautiful hand of one of the other prisoners: M. Martinez, Tim Hurley, and H. Wilson. The letter is on display at the Prison Museum.

Whereas, the departure of Mrs Frank S. Ingalls is near at hand, and we owe her our thanks, for the good work done in our behalf.

Be it resolved, that we the prisoners confined in this prison, attest our sincere thanks and appreciation, for the establishment of a Library, which has been to us a great source of enjoyment, and has also tended to improve us morally and intellectually, and further.

Be it resolved, that we thank and appreciate her attitude toward those whom she endeavored to cheer and comfort, while sick and in distress, further.

Be it resolved, that the good influences instilled by her kind work, shall prove to us in the future, as a stepping-stone to Society, and good Citizenship, and further.

Be it resolved, that by unanimous approval, a copy of these resolutions be handed to the Lady, in token of our high esteem.

Territorial Prison.
Yuma. Ariz.
April 5th 1886

Edward Reilly
Leon Levy
P. Wilson
Charles Miller
Alfred Brown

65

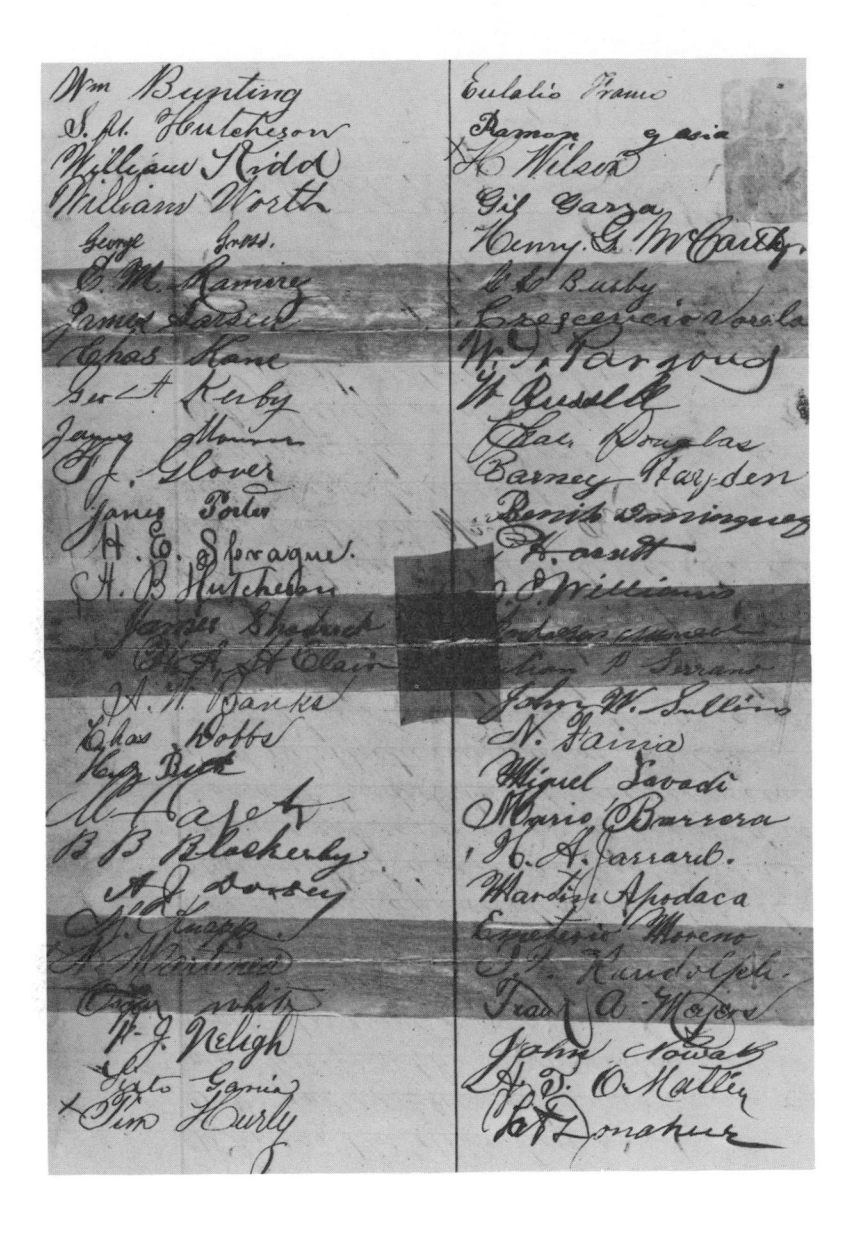

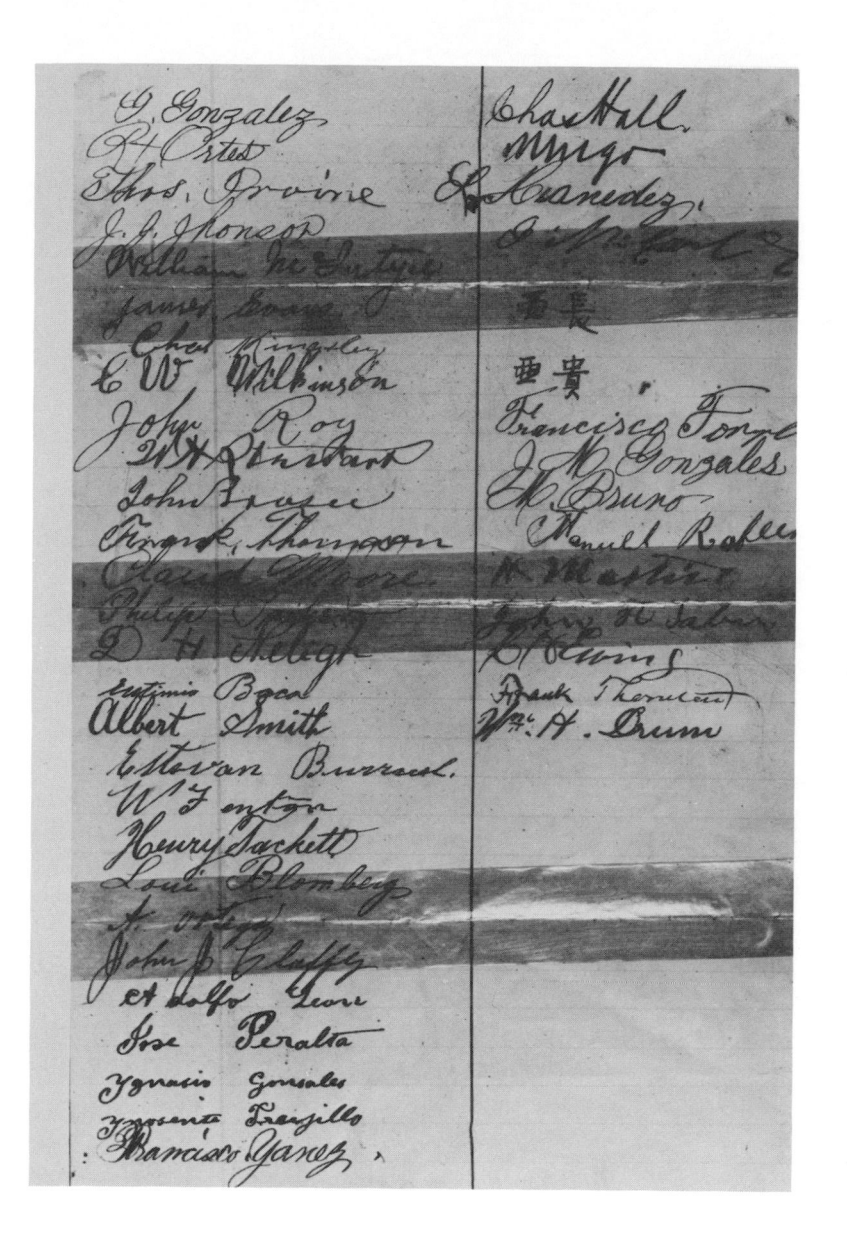

read or write when received by the prison, learned their letters here. One prisoner learned surveying. However, the classes were not universally popular, and the lack of funds contributed to the mediocre success of the educational efforts.

How might we summarize the 34 years contribution of the Arizona Territorial Prison? Somewhat out of the mainstream of the turbulent violence of other areas of Arizona, the Old Pen effectively contributed to the stabilizing of the territorial frontier. Without fanfare, with less funds than went into the construction of the walls of other prisons, with limited facilities, but with competent administrators and staff to set the standards for the administration, the history of the penitentiary does credit to its memory.

Prisoners in chow line, Main Yard. Note the conglomerate of prison uniforms. The fourth convict from the right looks almost dapper in his vertical stripes. (APHS)

CHAPTER IV
PRISONERS: APACHE RENEGADES
TO BANK PRESIDENT

EWER than 3,000 prisoners did penitence at this penitentiary. The first was William Mall, who wore the identification, No. 1. Mall began serving his term at the Yuma County Jail on May 20, 1875, before the prison on the hill was completed. Sentenced to life imprisonment for second degree murder, he was transferred to the prison when it was formally opened July 1, 1876.

The last prisoner to be sent to Yuma may have been Walter Sharp, No. 3056, sentenced to a life term for murder in 1909. He was transferred with many others to the new prison in Florence on August 29, 1909.

The convicts were numbered consecutively. Repeaters were given new numbers for subsequent terms. Since some were returned to the prison a second, third, fourth and even a fifth time, it is probable that the total of individual prisoners was closer to 3,000.

When a county sheriff or a federal marshal brought a prisoner up the steep, winding road to prison hill, he received a receipt signed by the superintendent or his assistant. A typical receipt read as follows:

No. 1737   Yuma, Arizona, April 14th, 1901

Received of Frank Murphy Sheriff of Pima County Isaac Field, convicted in the 1st Judicial District of the crime of Burglary first Degree and sentenced to be imprisoned in the Territorial Penitentiary at Yuma for the term of One Year.

                     Herbert Brown
                         Superintendent.

Caliche hillside at south side of Prison area, showing Guard Tower, ventilators, and the Women's Yard on the right separated from the Main Yard by a fence. The door to the Library may be seen to the left of the pole in the foreground. The shadow of the light fixture can be seen. (APHS)

The excitement of the trip to Yuma over, the newly arrived convict was immediately registered by the prison secretary or assistant superintendent.

For his name he received a number. His vital statistics were entered on a clean page of a large bound volume, one full page to a prisoner. Printed questions provided space for handwritten information. The sheets were large and the paper thick. There was a space for the convict's name, his cell assignment, the date of his receipt, registered number, alias, county, crime, sentence, nationality, education, race, legitimate occupation, height, complexion, color of hair, color of eyes, parents, religion, habits of life (whether temperate or intemperate), mental culture, use of tobacco, former imprisonment, name and address of nearest relative, peculiarity of build and features, beard worn when received, weight, and size of boot.

These questions and answers took about two-thirds of the

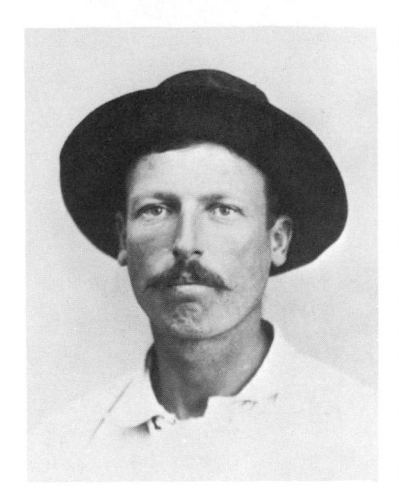

Unidentified prisoner. (YTPM)

Another train robber, Grant Wheeler, robbed train No. 20 on January 30, 1895, at Cochise. A one-time prisoner at the penitentiary, Wheeler poses here in a photographer's studio, with pistol and leather leggins. (YTPM)

12 x 14 page. The bottom area was left blank, and it was here that we find the chronological notations of prison life as in the record of an Apache Indian, Has Ral Te, No. 691: "May 30, 1893 confined in snake den 24 hours for refusing to work." Only one other notation graced the record of that poor Indian, who was received October 19, 1890: "April 1st/94. Died at 11 p.m., cause Consumption."

The newly-arrived prisoner, having had his wings clipped figuratively, now had his hair clipped literally. He was then photographed. In later years pictures were made both before and after the haircut, since usually the hairy, bearded or mustached convict bore little resemblance to the bald, pale, stark character in prison stripes.

71

He was given a bath and issued a prison uniform. In the early years of the prison the stripes were vertical, black and grey. In 1879 the stripes were made horizontal, and presumably for quicker recognition against the desert sand and brush, the colors were changed to black and yellow.

Prior to the turn of the century blue denims began to replace prison stripes, although stripes continued to be worn by some prisoners right up to the last. The Yuma prison apparently followed the common prison practice of keeping incorrigibles in stripes. The result was a conglomerate. Uniforms became faded and mismatched. A convict might wear pants with washed-out vertical black and grey stripes and a jacket with horizontal yellow and black stripes, or with no stripes at all. Topped by a floppy hat or cap, the effect was not dapper. The object was functional durability, not style.

In addition to the outer uniform, the prisoner was allowed one hat or cap, an extra pair of trousers, two pairs of drawers (underwear), two pairs of socks, two handkerchiefs, two towels, but only one pair of shoes.

He was allowed to have one toothpick, (that was the day of ivory toothpicks elegantly manipulated and sometimes secured on a fine gold chain), one tooth brush, and both a fine and a coarse comb. Photographs and other pictures of friends were approved. He was allowed mail which came through the prison office, a regular ration of tobacco, and could own books, with the requirement that his name be written plainly in ink across the printed matter in at least three places. He was issued two sheets and two pillow cases. Each article of clothing and bedding had to be conspicuously marked with his number.

Convicts were required to remain clean shaven, unless they could get special dispensation from the doctor or the superintendent. In a few cases this concession was granted.

Arizona in pioneer days was a melting pot and the prison inmates were an assorted lot.

Trades and occupations listed in the report of 1889 began with adobe layer and included blacksmith, basketmaker, bootblack, carpenter, cook, farmer, gambler, Indian scout, jockey, "Lady," plasterer, sailor, teamster, and wheelwrights. The largest numbers were laborers and "Indians Without Occupation."

Most of the states furnished felons who passed slowly through this prison, some coming from the New England, others from as far north as Michigan and Minnesota. Texas and New York supplied about the same number of native-born inmates as did Arizona, with California a good fourth.

Twenty-one foreign countries were represented at one time, and others at other times. Mexico supplied the majority of inmates during the years of prison operation, as more than half the prisoners confined at any period were Mexicans "born in Mexico." This apparent redundancy is necessary: in addition, there were American-born convicts of Mexican descent attributed to states of their birth.

From another continent, Scotland and Wales in the 1889 census contributed eight expatriates, and Ireland 29. Norway and Russia each contributed one, Germany eleven, England ten, and China twenty. Imported to work on railroads, the Chinese were victims of widespread anti-Oriental feelings in the West. They were seldom popular with other inmates and often miserable as prisoners. The unfortunate Quon Sing sought the solution to his troubles at Yuma in suicide.

The crimes for which the prisoners were convicted reveal the character of the frontier, a rugged but relatively uncomplicated environment. The 1889 official report is fairly representative of the era. Of 729 prisoners, only thirteen were convicted of "Offenses Against Public Morals." Ten of these were for polygamy or unlawful cohabitation, during a period when Mormons were being prosecuted, two for incest, and one for attempted abortion. Classified as "Offenses

Against Person," were five rapes and seven assaults with attempt to commit rape.

Several prisoners did time for robbing the U.S. mail, vio-
lating revenue laws, and selling liquor to Indians, but the
great bulk of the crimes were homicides, assaults, and robberies. A third of the total were listed simply as "Grand Larceny." Cattle rustling was not specifically identified, but
since this was widespread in Arizona late in the nineteenth
century, rustlers lucky enough to escape summary and more
severe punishment were listed in the larceny totals.

There were a few prisoners convicted of narcotic traffic,
some of them Chinese. The singular absence of emphasis on
dope, sex traffic, and perversion, is significant and remarkable when compared with penitentiaries in more developed
or sophisticated parts of the country, such as San Quentin in
California.

Of all the 3,000 prisoners at Yuma, fewer than one per-
cent were women. To nobody's surprise, these few women
caused as much trouble and received more publicity than
did the men. Their crimes were varied, but the kindest
thing any superintendent had to say about any of them was
that women were a terrible nuisance in a men's prison.

The names of the Indians even though unrecognized, stir
the imagination. Who has heard of Dil-z-hay, Ho-Chit, Nas
Good, Eu-das-dav-da, Bat Dish, or Say-es? These names
carry the aromatic suggestion of Arizona mountains and deserts but to all practical intents and purposes they are one
with Nineveh and Tyre. An Apache named Nah-Diz-Az
achieved a kind of immortality in the book *Apache Venge-
ance*. This unfortunate was confined for a time at the Arizona
Territorial Prison before being hanged. He was not exe-
cuted at the prison: No hangings ever took place there.

Apaches Say-es and Hos-col-te on October 18, 1890,
were sentenced to life imprisonment at Yuma for taking part
in the seizure of a stage coach which brought death to the

driver. In 3½ years Say-es was dead of tuberculosis. The prison record reports he died in cell 13.

A Mexican general and two members of his staff were sent to the Penitentiary, convicted of conspiring against Mexico. How or to what extent these educated men, distinguished in their own country, contributed to the great revolution which was then brewing in Mexico and erupted in 1910 (only suggested in the prison records), could be the subject of a chapter. Their efforts, however, involved two financiers from Bisbee, a bank president and a cashier, whose embezzlement was part of a plan to finance the forthcoming revolution.

Dr. R. R. Knotts, the last doctor at the Yuma prison, remembered the business men as "fine fellows personally, too." The doctor recounts that they had donned the prison uniform, and had submitted to their close hairclip, when one said to the other, "Say, boy, you look like hell in that outfit." This was the ex-cashier speaking to the ex-president. He looked up and saw Dr. Knotts. "Beg pardon," he said. The doctor replied, "No apology needed!" agreeing that it was indeed a hell of a place to be.

The record sheet of Adrianno Brinetti, No. 788, who was sentenced to serve two years in 1891 for grand larceny, although only twenty years old at the time, recalls he had not led a sheltered life. He admitted to intemperance, and was scarred by: "Bullet wound just below left knee." Two entries were added on his sheet after the descriptive material: "(1) solitary confinement for 24 hours for gambling; (2) discharged July 12, 1893, at expiration of sentence." His photograph indicates a nice-looking boy, and one wonders why he was required to serve his full sentence, when so many did not.

Panifilo Esparza, alias Francisco Hernandez, No. 3034, was described as having an "evil expression."

There is about as much harmony among convicts as honor

Panorama of the Prison, showing the limited and crowded area of Prison Hill. The Gatehouse and Sallyport in the center, and the Main Guard Station rising above the horizon in the left background, are the only buildings still remaining. (YTPM)

Prison swine yard in left foreground, with Prison Cemetery in middle background. Gila River in right background. This photograph was taken from Prison Hill looking southeast. (YTPM)

among thieves. Confinement, the oppressive proximity of so many steaming bodies, and a blasting-oven August contributed to a quarrel between two convicts serving life sentences one night in 1903. They were Simon Aldrate, from Iowa, and Francisco Garcia. The following morning Garcia stabbed Aldrate to death. Garcia was promptly tried in the District Court at Yuma, and was sentenced to hang. He was returned to the prison, and placed in solitary confinement pending the execution of his sentence.

The record of Jose Salazar bears witness to his weakness for gambling, and indirectly to its popularity in the prison. Four times, in June, August, September, and November, of 1891, he was caught gambling, and on the last two occasions was penalized with solitary confinement for a day. He was released after serving nineteen months of a two-year sentence.

The record of George Dwyer, No. 686, disclosed that he was a victim of the opium habit as well as a tobacco smoker. His crime was burglary and his sentence was five years. He was educated, and a tinner by occupation. He wore a full beard upon his receipt at Yuma in 1890. The record shows one punishment by confinement in the dark cell for 24 hours for fighting, and later that he was caught smuggling sulfate of morphine into the prison. He was then isolated from other prisoners. Reformation must have resulted, for he was pardoned in the fourth year of his sentence.

Juan Gutieriz was punished by solitary confinement for 24 hours for throwing a stone and hitting an Indian convict.

Bonita Domingues, No. 651, began his second term at Yuma in 1890. On November 25, 1891, he was adjudged insane by the Yuma probate judge and sent to Phoenix to the Territorial Insane Asylum. Five months later Bonita was released from the asylum and remanded to the prison. His final entry was written in a flowing, exquisite hand: "Died, December 2, 1892."

Charles Powers, No. 669, led an eventful life in prison. He only weighed 118 pounds, and unhesitatingly admitted that he drank, smoked and chewed. He made at least three attempts to escape, but despite that left the prison before the expiration of his five-year sentence with a full pardon and his citizenship restored. He first escaped on May 15, 1891, but was recaptured the next day at Gila Bend, the cost of his recapture to the Territory being $100.00. He escaped the following April 24, managing to avoid capture until May 8.

Charlie lost his good behavior credits and was punished by being required to wear a ball and chain and perform additional labor. In September he attempted escape again. During the day he concealed a ladder, (not easy to do anywhere, especially in a prison), intending to return after dark and scale the wall. Discovered before the zero hour, he had to wear a ball and chain for 90 days. But in 1894 things took an unexpectedly brighter turn for No. 669. All his credits were restored by resolution of the Board of Prison Commissioners, and he was pardoned by the Governor with restoration of his citizenship.

Three-Fingered Jack Laustenneau, No. 2029, was probably one of the most violent and vicious of the prison's incorrigibles. The burly Romanian labor agitator had been the leader in a strike of miners at Morenci in June of 1903. Had it not been for an act of God, a cloudburst on June 9, 1903, and the arrival of the Arizona National Guard the following day, Laustenneau might have become master of Morenci. He had organized 1,600 strikers into six military-like companies by persuading the men that his efforts had the support of both President Theodore Roosevelt of the United States and President Porfirio Diaz of Mexico. His conviction on a charge of riot was popular with most Arizona residents.

But prison could not restrain this brute of a man. A schemer and an organizer even behind prison walls, he was the leader in the savage break of April 28, 1904. When it

failed, and his agitation had not been subdued, solitary confinement appeared to be the only measure that promised the prison administration maximum security. In the end, it achieved what the company of his fellow man had not for Laustenneau. At least, the annual report of June 30, 1906 written by Assistant Superintendent Eugene Wilder said Three-fingered Jack was the only inmate to perish in the prison's Snake Den. The cause of his death was neither mistreatment, privation, nor poor accommodations. The prison doctor blamed Laustenneau's personal rage at his confinement, attributing death to apoplexy.

Buckskin Frank Leslie was the most colorful frontiersman to do time at the pen. He got his name from the fringed buckskin coat that he affected in Tombstone during its wildest and most vicious days. While he was one of the notorious bad men of Arizona, he was respected by some for qualities of relative merit and social value.

For one thing, Leslie had a visible and honorable means of support. He was a bartender at the Oriental Bar, by no means the lowest rung on the social ladder of Tombstone in that era. He was an excellent tracker and had served the U.S. Army in that capacity on the chase for Geronimo. As a gunman he was compared to Doc Holliday in marksmanship. Soon after his arrival at Tombstone, after an evening of refreshment and amusement at a saloon with the winsome Mary Galeen, and while escorting the lady home (the record is not clear whether to hers or his), Buckskin Frank was fired upon by Mary's husband. Tombstone tradition insists that although the assailant was high above street level on a balcony, and there was only desert moonlight to aim by, Buckskin Frank shot the man between the eyes. That his intentions were honorable might be suggested by the fact that he married the widow Galeen shortly after the fatal encounter with her husband. In time Mary divorced him, and married a man with less talent with a gun, complaining to

friends that Frank once had her stand against the wall of their room while he fired bullet after bullet at her outline.

Suspected by some of killing the notorious Johnny Ringo while the latter was sleeping off a drunk, he was said to have killed several men. He was acquitted of the shooting of Billy Claibourne as a matter of obvious self defense. Finally, in a fit of jealousy while drunk he killed Molly Bradshaw, lady of the night and his sometime sweetheart. He was convicted of her murder and sentenced to a term of 25 years. He was a good prisoner, and served only seven of them, much of the time as the doctor's chief assistant in the prison infirmary. He was released in 1897, and thereafter only briefly and occasionally was his apparently uneventful existence noted.

Gov. Benjamin J. Franklin, in recommending pardon for Buckskin Frank, made a strong case to the 19th Legislative Assembly on January 28, 1897:

Pardon [is] strongly recommended by the present and late prison officials on the ground of exemplary conduct and valuable services. Dr. [P. G.] Cotter, late prison physician, states that during epidemics when his assistance to the sick deprived Leslie of his rest night-and-day for weeks at a time, he never murmured but was a most humane and self sacrificing attendant.

His pardon was further recommended by many prominent citizens, Territorial Officials and United States Army officers. Lieutenant Colonel Lawler, of the United States Army, writes that Arizona was terrorized by the atrocities of the hostile Indian tribes, under Geronimo, Mr. Leslie was the first to respond to a call for assistance, and gave splendid service to the army as a scout and guide.

He is shown to be a man of good character and education, his only fault being that he occasionally drinks to excess, and was crazed by drink when he committed this crime.

I am assured that he has entirely abstained from the use of intoxicating liquors, and although submitted to the strongest temptation as a prison druggist, has never betrayed a trust . . .

Before leaving the prisoners, at least a part of the story of the women prisoners should be touched upon.

In all there were only a few more than two dozen women who did time at the prison. Five were in custody in 1909, when all inmates were transferred to Florence, but none were of any particular interest. Earlier women prisoners did leave their mark on Arizona, however.

The most notorious was Pearl Hart, even though she never lived up to her publicity. Pearl's only recorded contribution to crime was the amateurish holdup of the Globe stage. Her confederate in the fiasco was one Joe Boot. The stickup itself came off reasonably well even if Joe and Pearl were nervous, but the not-very-smart team had not given enough thought to their getaway. Their capture was a matter of degrading simplicity to the sheriff of Pinal County.

Pearl, with a naughty eye to the Big Chance, which came off only slightly better than her hold-up, made the most of the publicity that followed her arrest. A lady stage coach robber was a novelty to the news-hungry yellow press. Reporters and magazine writers, carried away by the mystique of a female Black Bart, converted her into a veritable veteran of crime. She was credited with rail and stage robberies which were wholly imaginary. Mention of the possibilities of a stage career, (the "legitimate" stage) caught Pearl's fancy. She cooperated willingly, if ham-ily, by frequent posturings, with truculent underlip. Many pictures were taken of Pearl presenting heavy pistols toward imaginary victims, or lounging comfortably with one booted foot on an upturned bucket, a lever action rifle cradled in her arm.

Most of the excitement surrounding Pearl came before her conviction—for possession of a stolen pistol. On the charge of stage robbery her associate was convicted and Pearl was acquitted, but the judge was not influenced by the flip-flap of Pearl's flirtations directed to an all-male and awe-struck jury. He ordered her tried on the second charge and off to Yuma she went.

Prisoner Pearl Hart in baggy men's clothing. (APHS)

Seated demurely in a Captain's Chair, one can guess why Pearl Hart was a disrupting influence at the Territorial Prison, a maximum security penitentiary for men.

(APHS)

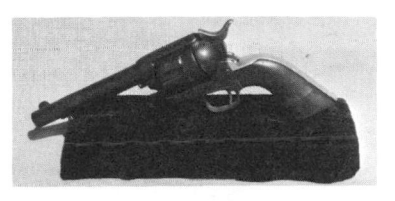

Pistol now in the Prison Museum, which belonged to Pearl Hart. Her name is engraved on the buttplate.

Dr. R. R. Knotts, the last doctor at the Arizona Territorial Prison, shown here as a Captain in the Medical Corps of the Army. (YTPM)

At the Territorial Prison she was an attraction, no doubt of it, and a favorite of guards and staff. Nobody seemed to mind when Joe Boot escaped on February 6, 1901, least of all Pearl, who had branded him a coward for not putting up a fight when the two were captured. Pearl's feminine wiles were to win her freedom with an unexpected parole on December 15, 1902, some months before she had served minimum time that would have qualified her for release. Fifty years after the fact the man who had been Governor Alexander O. Brodie's secretary revealed that Pearl had been released from the prison to avoid a scandal threatened by the prison physician's report that she was expecting a baby. She had departed for the Midwest to fulfill the dreams of a stage career before anybody thought to confirm the medical prognosis.

Elana Estrada, lacking self-discipline at a moment of crisis when betrayed by her boy friend, was not satisfied with his death. She might have gotten away with killing him, but she went too far. Elana cut out his heart. Worse, she slammed it in his face. This disturbed her peers, and Elana wound up for a short stay at the Old Pen.

Bertha Trimble had the unique distinction of being the only woman sent to the penitentiary for rape.

Manuela Fiebres, convicted of murdering a Chinese in Tucson, arrived at the prison at the age of twenty. At first she was prudently segregated from the other convicts by Superintendent Ingalls. However, when he was succeeded as warden by Johnny Behan, she was given the run of the prison. As rapidly as the laws of nature permitted, Manuela contributed two wards to increase the growing population of the Territory.

Miss May Woodman and the man she killed were both victims of a practical joker. The *Tombstone Epitaph* published an item supplied by some anonymous joker to the effect that one William Kinsman was soon to marry Miss May

Woodman. Not realizing that by so doing he was putting his life on the line, Kinsman paid for an ad in which he disclaimed any such matrimonial intention. The record is silent as to the relationship between the two, but evidently Miss Woodman felt aggrieved, and she wished him dead. In such matters with May Woodman to think was to act. She shot him dead the same day in front of the Crystal Palace Gambling Saloon. Well liked by the other prisoners and members of the staff, May made no trouble other than that occasioned by the presence of a woman in what was essentially a man's prison. Although given a life sentence, she had served less than three years when she was pardoned and disappeared.

Fanny King was a Tonto Apache, her crime forgotten. Isabelle Washington, received at the prison in 1883 and Pearl Eiker in 1907, both for manslaughter, and Ada Parks in 1908, for grand larceny, were Negroes. Theresa Garcia and Saferina Garcia, not related, Class of '96 and '08 respectively. Maria Morena, Allegricia de Otero, Eulogia Bracamonte, and Rosa Duran, apparently were of Mexican extraction, and had committed such social errors as manslaughter, selling liquor to Indians, assault with a deadly weapon, and grand larceny. Exie Sedgmore assaulted someone with a deadly weapon, and was in turn assaulted with a sentence of three years. She was pardoned in two months, which probably is a story in itself. A Mrs. E. M. Bridford drew six years in 1909, and was among those transferred to Florence. Two little angels, Angelita Verdusco and Angelita Sonoqui, were chastened with ten months and six months each for adultery.

Women at the Old Pen were few, and none of them stayed very long. Invariably administrations labored to gain them early pardons and paroles. This was not the frontier type of chivalry: the fact is that the ladies were, administratively speaking, poison.

The term "lifer" is used to designate a convict who re-

ceives a life sentence, or one of 99 years. What happened to such men at Yuma? The surprising fact is that they served less time on an average than did criminals convicted of lesser crimes. A very few served several years, but as of an 1890 report, the average sentence actually served by these lifers was less than three years. Practically all surviving lifers were pardoned, including the Indians. The average length of their sentences was reduced by the ultimate punishment in cases where death came soon, often from tuberculosis. They did better, as a whole, than those who had received five and ten-year sentences for attempted murder or assault.

A great many of the convicts, not just the lifers, were pardoned sooner or later. Some pardons came either on the day or a few days before the prisoner had served his term. The intent and the effect in these cases was to restore citizenship to the convict for his return to society.

Seventeen prisoners were paroled during the two years prior to July 1, 1904, and 29 convicts were pardoned. Twenty-one of these were pardons to restore citizenship, and the other eight were pardons substantially shortening terms.

There were about 3,000 prisoners at the Old Pen and 3,000 stories.

John Thomson, alias "Kid" Thomson, was a train robber and a prisoner at the Old Pen. He held up and robbed the Southern Pacific Express Train at Roscos, California, in December 1893. (YTPM)

Juan Zavala was a Guard at the Prison. His name may be found upon the records also spelled as Zabala. (YTPM)

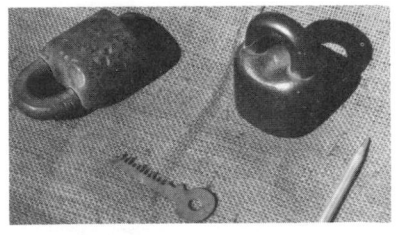

Padlocks used at the Prison, now on display at the Museum.

Handcuffs used at the Penitentiary now on display in the Prison Museum.

Heavy leg irons which by their weight and short length of chain inhibited rapid movement. On display at the Prison Museum.

Ball and chain on display at Prison Museum.

Leg irons, and two sets of handcuffs, used on prisoners at the Territorial Prion, and now on display at the Prison Museum. Note improved ratchet-type version in upper right.

CHAPTER V
ESCAPES AND BREAKS

HEY say that during warm spring days, after a night of hearing honking geese passing northward, the Old Pen at Yuma pulsated with an undercurrent of suppressed excitement. At such times the guard was doubled as the assistant superintendent racked his brain to devise diversionary duties to ease the mounting tension of men confined in the sun-seared prison. Checking the safety catches of their rifles and pressing their palms heavily and comfortably against the sidearms they wore, the guards walked their posts on top of the high wall with extra caution. The prison had no record of a major break, but among its inmates were men who lived reckless lives.

The chief mission of a maximum security prison is to hold its prisoners. Likewise, the dominating and central thought of nearly every convict is escape; if not that, at least freedom is his unwavering hope, although, strange as it might seem, some few of the prisoners appeared perfectly happy and content under confinement.

The Territorial Prison at Yuma was no exception to the general rule. Many convicts tried to leave before their prison terms had expired. Opportunity, whether contrived or accidental, is an essential element of successful escape. Inside the walls prisoners had little opportunity. It was outside, on working parties or as trusties performing some chore, that all of the successful escapes from Yuma originated.

One of the myths of the Arizona Territorial Prison is that no prisoner—or only one—ever escaped. This is untrue. A considerable number escaped over the period of 34 years.

The State Prison at Florence maintains file folders on territorial prisoners as well as custody of the old Prisoners

Ledgers. These ledgers carry the notation of each escape, and the file folders are flagged with small red tabs fastened to the top edge and are stamped on the outside "ES-CAPED," where the prisoner is still at large. The youngest of these men would be about 80 years old if still living, and in some cases, well over 100. Their files are still not closed.

In a sense the Territorial Prison was escape-proof: No break from inside the prison walls ever succeeded, nor did any prisoner successfully escape from a locked cell.

There were probably less than half a dozen prison breaks, concerted and open attempts at escape accompanied by violence. An exact number is difficult to establish; some possibly were never recorded. Others may have been reported in the laconic style of officialdom, without emphasis as to violence, concealed in superintendents' reports as undetailed statistics.

Considering the almost 34 years of prison operation, and the fact that accommodations were not ideal but usually cramped, the wonder is that there were not more breaks. Obviously "firm but not Draconian" discipline and the readiness of alert, capable guards to take whatever steps were necessary to subdue trouble constituted an extremely powerful deterrent. The guards were not harsh, and they were strictly enjoined from abusing or manhandling convicts, but they also were instructed to use instant force to stop an escape or put down a riot.

All guards wore pistols. Standing solidly above them was the lethal Battery in the guard tower. But even more, the "gun that won the West," the 44-40 Winchester lever action repeating rifle, ruled the prison and accounted for most convicts brought down in escapes.

Except for incorrigibles or those receiving special punishment in the Snake Den, prisoners had the run of the prison during the day, limited by the walls or by their work assignments. Prisoners who had demonstrated a capacity for

dependability were made trusties, and were permitted to leave the prison grounds on prison business unattended. More than one trusty, drinking the sweet air of freedom, found himself unable to resist an opportunity for flight.

Groups of prisoners in work parties labored on the rock hill, the prison farm, the wood yard, Yuma city streets, and on other projects, watched by armed guards. There were escapes from working parties despite constant vigilance.

Most maximum security penitentiaries have a history of riots with inmates revolting against bad food, bad treatment, or other real or imagined grievances. The Territorial Prison at Yuma records no riot involving any substantial number of its convicts.

For ten years the prison record was unblemished until October of 1887 the first and the most important break took place. Seven convicts were involved, all Mexicans. The excitement lasted not over two or three minutes, but the outburst ended with four prisoners killed, another wounded, and the superintendent so badly wounded that he never recovered and eventually committed suicide as a result of the unending pain he suffered. The story of the break as told by Superintendent Thomas Gates would lose color and vividness by any words other than his own:

As I started to leave the paint shop to go to the north Sallyport, Lopez, (a prisoner) who was working in the shoe shop, walked up to me, stating that he had not been let out of the corridor as early as had previously been the case and that since he was anxious to learn the trade of shoemaking, desired to know the reason . . . about this time, we had reached the north Sallyport of the wall where Puebla Vasquez and Bustamente surrounded me. Puebla . . . and Lopez, who could speak good English, explained that if I would escort them to the Gila River brush lying to the east side of the river, and order the Guards not to fire, they would not harm me, but I had the power to give them their liberty and that if I failed to do so, or if anyone of their number was hurt, I should have to die.

Bacca, Padilla and Villa ordered the Gate Keeper who was a convict, to throw open the gates, with which order he complied. The trio then dashed over to the Superintendent's house and demanded arms . . . and assaulted Yardmaster Fredley (who was unarmed) with a pick. In the struggle the two fell over the steep enbankment on the west side, Fredley being the uppermost.

Assistant Superintendent J. H. Behan in the meantime closed the gates, taking the keys from the Gate Keeper, and then went to the Superintendent's house to obtain arms. He then passed to the west side of the wall and taking a rifle from Guard J. C. Cotter, passed on to the assistance of Fredley, and brought back Padilla.

Bacca then ran around the north side of the Superintendent's house towards the Colorado River but was halted by Guard E. O. Williams. Villa ran down on the road on the west side of the wall, carrying a bag of provisions. Fire was opened upon him by Guard W. H. Reynolds, who was stationed on the southwest corner of the wall. The convict slipped over a steep bank out of range of fire, where he remained until after the melee was over, but he was brought back to the Prison and was found to have received two bullets through the shoulder and arm.

Puebla, who was the leader, searched me for weapons, and finding none, ordered Bustamente to tie my hands . . . As we marched out of the Sallyport towards the office, Vasquez and Lopez were in front, Puebla on my left side, and Bustamente on my right, the two latter holding me fast.

Lopez and Vasquez, in the meantime, had rushed into the office where they broke open my desk and took my pistol, which contained five loads.

Just at this time, I signaled Guard B. F. Hartlee, who was stationed on the main stand near the northeast corner of the wall, to fire . . . His first shot was at Villa as he ran around the northwest corner of the wall. Lopez ran up to me and leveled the pistol at me. I knocked the weapon to one side with my hand, when it was discharged, the bullet passing through . . . Puebla's arm.

Secretary Rule at this moment appeared upon the scene and

struck Puebla over the head with a revolver, stunning him a little, but not sufficiently to break his grasp upon me. Rule and Lopez fired at each other at the same instant, both missing. Rule then ran . . . Lopez followed.

Guard Hartlee shot Lopez down, and as the latter raised up, shot him again. He fell, and Rule, coming up again, shot Lopez through the arm, and went into the office. Hartlee shot Busta-mente, who first making a cut at me with his knife broke away and staggering, fell near the north side of the Sallyport.

Vasquez, who was Puebla's associate at the time, was the next to fall with the crack of Hartlee's rifle. Puebla, who had kept me between himself and Hartlee, drove his butcher knife . . . into my body near my neck . . .

Still grasping me (the knife being still in my body), he stepped backward, pulling me, his object probably being to gain a point on the west side of the office, where, being out of range of Hartlee's fire, he would be able to escape to the Colorado River.

At this juncture Barney Riggs, a life convict, seeing me be-tween the two convicts before the firing commenced, and be-lieving me to be trying to separate the men who he thought were fighting each other, ran out to assist me. When the shooting commenced, he dodged around the west side of the office and remained standing there.

Seeing Riggs, I ordered him to get the pistol from Lopez, and shoot Puebla who was stabbing me. Riggs at once jerked up and out of Lopez's hand and shot Puebla near the heart. The shot caused the latter to pull the knife from the wound with such force that it flew over his head more than ten feet and caused him to break loose from me.

Hartlee then shot him once more, through the small of the back, Riggs also firing a bullet through his thigh before he fell. This convict was the first to die, living only about thirty minutes.

I staggered and Riggs caught me by the arm while another convict named Sprague, placing his hand over the wound to prevent the blood escaping, assisted me to my room . . .

Guard Hartlee does not know to this day why it was that he did not kill convict Riggs, as he had the latter covered by the

rifle and knew him to be a life convict, but something seemed to tell him not to shoot. Had he killed Riggs, Puebla would certainly have killed me.

Puebla, Bustamente, Lopez and Vasquez, were all dead before sunset that day. I don't think the fight lasted over two minutes. As a result of the attempt to escape, in which none of the participants succeeded, in addition to the four convicts being killed, another Villa was wounded, being struck by two bullets.

Superintendent Gates was never to fully recover from his stab wounds. On the second regular meeting of the Prison Commissioner in April 1888, he resigned owing to ill health. Assistant Superintendent John H. Behan, who had been sheriff of Cochise County during its bloodiest days, was chosen to succeed him, and Guard B. F. Hartlee was temporarily elevated to assistant superintendent.

Two years later, in 1890, Superintendent Frank Ingalls recapitulated escapes for the fifteen years since establishment of the Territorial Prison, listing convicts that had not been recaptured as of December 31, 1890. They totalled only seven.

J. Lewis, No. 21, was the first to escape. He slipped away on December 11, 1878, no doubt to enjoy a pleasant Chirstmas season. Theodore Brown, No. 20, made good his flight a month later, January 13, 1879.

There were no further effective escapes for four years, but two convicts escaped in 1883, one in 1885, and two more in 1889.

The first prisoner to be killed while attempting to escape was Jose M. Ramirez, who made a break for liberty with seventeen other prisoners working in the prison graveyard, December 28, 1885. Superintendent Ingalls himself brought the Lowell Battery, a type of Gatling gun, into play, subduing fifteen of the men. Ramirez lost his life, another prisoner was captured later, and one convict made a clean getaway over the Sonoran border.

Five prisoners in all were killed in escape attempts during the fifteen-year period, Ramirez and the four named by Gates in the 1887 break. There were to be more.

In his report for the calendar year of 1890, Superintendent Ingalls indicated:

The discipline of the prisoners, barring a few minor infringements of rules, which are promptly checked and punished by confinement in the dark cell, leaves nothing to be wished . . . The solitary exception being the escape of two prisoners—Keys and Warrell—on the evening of November 23rd, by scaling the south side wall. Fortunately both were recaptured, punished by confinement in the dark cell, made to carry a ball and chain, and reported to the Board of Commissioners, as provided for in . . . the statutes.

Nowhere in official reports did the superintendent mention the attempt of Pedro Yanes to separate himself from the Old Pen. To the *Arizona Sentinel* we are indebted for the article from its April 19, 1890 issue:

About two o'clock, Thursday afternoon, Pedro Yanes, a convict from Graham County, who was engaged in wheeling wood to the pump house at the Territorial Prison, was found to have effected an escape. His trail was found by Indian trailers, on the Mesa west of town, and Guards Frank King and Selmo Figeroa followed it up. In the meantime, Assistant Superintendent B. F. Hartlee struck across the County heading for the Sonora Road. Friday morning at ten o'clock they overtook the would-be escape ten miles above Gila City. Mr. Hartlee took in the foot-sore convict and soon had him ensconsed behind bars again. It is thought that Yanes managed to elude the Guard by jumping into the river from the pump house, which is on the water's edge, and kept under the water until he drifted to the guard station, then landing, made for the road, following which he was captured.

Undoubtedly there were many such dramatic incidents that have never been vignetted, and which have been lacon-

ically reported or never officially reported at all. We can imagine for reasons of prison politics, kindness, or even the nuisance of the paperwork involved, that some such incidents and violations went unheralded.

William Harris, No. 736, was one of four or five prisoners who attempted escape in 1892. All were immediately retaken. Two of these men tried twice, such was their drive for freedom. A particularly illuminating glimpse of prison procedures at the time appeared in an article in the *Arizona Sentinel* of May 11, 1892.

ALL CAPTURED

Thos. Wicks, one of the prison guards, captured Forrest and Govero, two of the three prisoners that escaped from the prison April 24, at Tacna, the Mexican having been captured near the Andrade place at the boundary line. After his capture the other two at once set out for town, where they were trailed by the Indian runners, and also followed by the guards, to the railroad water tank, where they took the work-train and went to La Gerta. From there they walked to Tacna, where guard Wicks held them up.

In 1895 and 1896 there were fourteen escape attempts, all by trusties. Nine were recaptured and returned to prison, being at liberty but a short time. Of the five who remained at large, two escaped while employed on the prison farm, two while working at the wood camp, and one from the immediate vicinity of the prison. These lucky escapers were Manuel Bacca, Catana Vasquez, Henry Ferguson, Thomas Cameron, and Joe Dace.

During 1899 and the first six months of 1900, there was a rash of escape attempts. A full dozen attempted to flee in 1899, three on April 11, and two August 28. All but one, Hank Halen, No. 1360, were recaptured.

January 18, 1900, was marked by the escape of Mose Gibson, No. 1521, and two Indians, Apache Es-Kay-

No-E, No. 1403, and Navajo Hosteen Nes, No. 1420. Mose and Es-Kay-No-E enjoyed liberty for only three days, whereas it was almost seven months later, August 7, that Hosteen Nes was collared.

On March 14, 1900, four Mexicans and John Gatlan, No. 1504, made a break. Four were captured, and Miguel Guardiola, No. 1480, was shot. He died two days later.

Escape must have been in the air that spring, for on May 21 Gatlan made a second unsuccessful attempt, and the next day four other prisoners attempted to escape without success. But the spirit of escape was rampant. Two days later, John McKinley, No. 1499, was brought down in attempted flight by a well-placed shot in the left ankle.

The case history of Garbino Lopez was more detailed than most. On June 17, 1891, he was received as No. 741 for the crime of robbery. He was only eighteen years old, entering on a seven-year sentence. Garbino said he was half Mexican and half Yaqui. He weighed only 130 pounds, but every pound was wildcat.

Six weeks after his arrival, Garbino made his first attempt to escape in company with a convict named Francisco Lopez. The record doesn't reveal that they were related. At that time a gang of twenty-one convicts was assigned to work on the levee bordering the east side of Yuma, and was being marched out in charge of guards, Mike Rice and John Martin. Rice was in front of the line. Martin brought up the rear. The Lopez boys were at the head of the line of prisoners. When they reached the southern point of Prison Hill they jumped on Rice, quickly wresting away his rifle. As Francisco levered a cartridge into the rifle chamber, Rice cooly drew his pistol and shot him on the left side above the hip. Both convicts then ran along the dusty road toward the levee. Rice followed, pausing from time to time to shoot.

Guards on the tower, alerted by the firing, turned the Gatling Gun on the running men, who had reached the levee.

Yuma Prison Cemetery. Prison Hospital center, top. (APHS)

Francisco, already wounded, was weakening. He fell to his knees after running about 300 yards along the levee. Guard B. F. Hartlee was waiting at the levee for the men to go to work. Unarmed, but alert, he borrowed the dumbfounded Martin's pistol and joined the chase. Garbino Lopez, although willing to risk rifle fire and the Gatling Gun, surrendered as soon as he saw he was being followed by Hartlee. Although both might have been shot dead on the spot for the assault on Rice, they were spared. Francisco was found to have only a flesh wound. Garbino was fitted with a ball-and-chain.

Back on a work gang by January 26 of the following year, and longing for his wild, free mountains, Garbino tried again and this time got away. When others of the levee gang were lined up to march to dinner, he hid in an excavation from which dirt for the levee had been obtained. When the convicts were counted at the prison gate, Garbino was found missing. Guards Ward and Wilder started on his trail. Two days later they captured him at Adonde, 30 miles east of

96

Yuma, after a night of drenching rain and cold had taken nearly all the spirit out of Garbino. His punishment was 30 days in the Snake Den.

Garbino's punishment again failed to convince him of the error of his ways. Four months later he made a third attempt to escape, this time hiding in the yard, avoiding the evening lockup, and scaling the wall during the night. His record does not reveal where he was recaptured, but at 2 o'clock the next morning he was collared by reliable Guard Hartlee. Again fitted with ball and chain, he was given additional labor on the road gang.

The Board of Commissioners on July 7, 1892, recognized the need of making an example of Garbino. By resolution they cancelled all of his credits prior to his recapture on March 27. Never again was Garbino Lopez to make an escape attempt or breathe the air of Arizona as a free man. In June 1893 he was given 24 hours in solitary confinement for gambling. Two months later Garbino Lopez was found dead on the floor of his cell in the hot early hours before sunrise. Death was attributed to "paralysis of the heart." Never to see his twenty-first birthday, the boy was buried in the prison cemetery on August 26th, 1893. In accordance with custom, the American flag that could be seen from almost any point in Yuma was lowered to half mast, a last tribute to a convict never to leave the Prison. It acknowledged that while Garbino Lopez was a felon, he was also a man. A rough headboard marked his grave, bearing the stark inscription, No. 741.

During the administration of Superintendent Frank S. Griffith, there were three attempts to escape from the prison during the two-year period from July 1st, 1902 to June 30, 1904.

The first attempt, according to the Superintendent's Report, was made during the noon hour on January 9, 1903, when the guards were letting out trusties to attend to their

various duties. The attempt was promptly frustrated. One of the wall guards shot a would-be-escaper, and another guard was wounded.

On March 6, 1903, a second attempt was made. Prisoners were being marched to work after dinner when two broke from the ranks and ran for the gate. The guards repeatedly called on the two to stop, and finally fired, bringing them down. Both died of their wounds. If there had been a planned concerted escape, it was aborted by the prompt and effective gunfire.

The last big dramatic break of the prison before its closing was the climax of the series in Griffith's administration, and occurred in 1904. We find a phenomenon repeated: Again a prisoner came to the rescue of the superintendent, hardly an act calculated to increase his popularity or life expectancy within the walls. It suggests that the superintendent was respected, that by no means were all prisoners desperados, and that some good—perhaps much good—was accomplished at the Old Pen.

Superintendent Griffith told of the break in an official report:

On the morning of April 28, 1904, a party of convicts assaulted the (Assistant) Superintendent and myself, inside the yard, with the view of using our bodies for shields, while the men escaped through the gate and took possession of the Armory.

What would have been a very serious break was frustrated by the promptness of the Guard Stevens in obeying orders to shoot regardless of the presence of officials. Three of the rioters were wounded, and the Assistant Superintendent also received buck shot in the leg, and a knife thrust from one of the prisoners.

Fifteen men were involved in this break, and much of the credit for putting it down was due to the prison cook, a convict, W. T. Buck. He ran to the rescue of the superintendent and assistant superintendent armed only with a large

kitchen knife. He jumped between Griffith and the convicts, receiving a stab intended for the warden. Although wounded, Buck continued to fight until the break was quelled.

Convicts involved in the attempt were placed in solitary confinement, pending trial, and Buck was later pardoned for his courageous action.

The Arizona Territorial Prison was not escape-proof, since necessarily some of its operations were carried on by convicts beyond the close confines of its walls. It proved to be practically break-proof, when the attempts were made within the walls.

Certainly the Territorial Prison does not suffer by being compared with penitentiaries of its day, in considering both personal relations and the relative lack of malevolent violence. Superintendent Johnny Behan, although not the ablest administrator in its history, is credited with personally undertaking the capture of an escaped convict because he feared his subordinate might kill the man unnecessarily.

An essential truth that contributed to the remarkable record of this frontier prison is found in the explanation of why an armed, escaped convict, overtaken at a lonely place, had not killed the guard trailing him. He had surrendered without a struggle. "Sure, I could have killed him—but he was my friend."

Beautiful inlaid wooden box, in casing carving set, painstakingly created by prisoner, on display at the Museum.

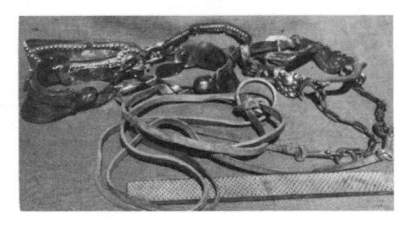

Bridle made by one of the prisoners, with rasp for scale. Both are on display at the Museum.

99

CHAPTER VI
THE END OF AN ERA AND A PRISON

HE ruins on Prison Hill are only a remainder of the extensive facilities which were abandoned that night, on September 15, 1909, when the last 40 prisoners were shackled together and marched down from Prison Hill to the train that was to take them to the new prison at Florence.

From the first day to the last, during the whole of the 34 years of its activity, growth of the prison population required additional and enlarged facilities. These were added from time to time until all available space was taken and some of the prison buildings even encroached on property not belonging to the Territory.

By 1909 the increasing pressures for more room made some change mandatory, and the only question then was whether other property be found for the new prison in Yuma or elsewhere in the Territory. The inland town of Florence, where Deputy Sheriff Joe Phy was killed in a gunfight with Pete Gabriel, became the location for the new larger, modern, establishment. But it is with those hot, dusty years of growing pains for the Arizona Territory and its prison that we have been interested.

The prison made valuable contributions in those early years in such practical ways as development of electricity and farming, and experiments with manufacture and industry. The prison is said to have had one of the first light plants west of Chicago. In spite of stringent economies, prison authorities experimented with pumping facilities, blowers to ventilate the cells, etc.

Convict labor was used for practically everything, and some of the work was of the hardest type, such as excavating the granite hills and breaking rocks. Some convicts found employment in the shops, and others were assigned house-keeping and administrative work. Private industry sought convict labor. Such labor was exploited in many states. Ari-zonians considered this a degrading form of slavery, and it was not for them. One such contract was made in 1897, but it was unsuccessful and short lived. Another contract was en-tered into by the Board of Prison Commissioners, but the Governor and the Superintendent refused to permit the prisoners to be used for such a purpose, and it did not take the Territory Administration long to rally around that stand.

All this was building experience and character in the peo-ple of the Territory, and much was contributed by the Prison Administration. This was a period when scandals rocked penitentiaries around the country, and rocked and re-rocked San Quentin in neighboring California; but during the en-tire 34 years of its operation, the Yuma Prison Administra-tion was not involved in a serious scandal, and never had a real riot.

Prisoners were handled humanely and in an enlightened manner that still is an accepted standard for the great major-ity of penitentiaries in the United States. The worst punish-ment offered was solitary confinement, (administered by to-day's prisons as "isolation") on bread and water, possibly with a ball and chain. One superintendent stated that the convicts did not come to the Penitentiary to be punished, but as punishment. The punishment of solitary confinement was reserved to those who broke the prison rules, and for incor-rigibles. The interesting thing is that almost everywhere else in the United States corporal punishment was the rule rather than the exception. The refined tortures of the San Quentin Overcoat, murderous floggings, and other shocking prac-tices, were employed by most prison administrations. In ad-

Territorial Prison as seen on skyline from Madison Street railroad bridge. (APHS, Reynolds Collection)

Another view of the southwest corner, showing the Prison Hospital in the upper center. The Hospital, no doubt the most comfortable place during hot weather in the Prison, was on the second floor over the Cell Block. (YTPM)

dition to those barbarities, San Quentin during this period used the Water Cure where the unfortunate convict is battered by a heavy stream of water under high pressure, spread-eagled in the same manner as in the flogging, but facing the hose. Other prisons had other tortures, some attributable to the sadism of the warden, but for the most part misguided attempts to maintain order. Some states still impose disciplinary measures such as the "Sweat Box," "Cage Door," and other brutalities, but Yuma never did. Nor could it be maintained that the inmates at Yuma could be considered a gentler variety than might be found in these other prisons.

Whether all this was planned or fortuitous, the net effect was the increase of stature of the Territory.

There were breaks for freedom, and these desperate men attacked and at least on three occasions threatened the lives of the superintendents or his staff. The interesting thing about this is, not that they tried to escape, for escapes are incident to all prisons, and not that they attacked their guards, for this cannot always be avoided in escape attempts. The curious fact is that, except on one break, the escapees refused to kill in order to make good their escape. In the three instances mentioned, the escapes were aborted and the lives of the superintendent and his assistants were saved by other prisoners who came to their rescue. This would appear to be at least an endorsement of the humanitarianism of the administrations, and suggests the degree of regard and respect in which they were held by the prisoners.

All this is not to say that all the superintendents were equally good, or that all of them were good. Some of them were excellent, and they fortunately set the tone generally for the Prison. The others suffered in comparison with the better superintendents. It was Superintendent Johnny Behan, for example, who received heavy criticism for allowing prisoner Manuella Fiebres to become pregnant twice in two years. In this he was unfavorably compared with Superin-

The following Menu is part of the report of Superintendent Ingalls for the period ending December 31, 1890, the first Territorial Prison report since its inception in 1876.

DAILY BILL OF FARE

SUNDAY

Breakfast: Fresh beef hash, wheat bread and coffee.
Supper: Roast beef, mashed potatoes, soup, wheat bread, pie and tea.

MONDAY

Breakfast: Bacon and beans, bread and coffee.
Dinner: Bacon and beans, bread.
Supper: Fruit, rice, bread and coffee.

TUESDAY

Breakfast: Beefsteak, potatoes, bread and coffee.
Dinner: Pot-pie, made with potatoes and onions.
Supper: Beef stew, bread and coffee.

WEDNESDAY

Breakfast: Beefsteak, boiled potatoes, bread and coffee.
Dinner: Roast beef, beans and bread.
Supper: Onion stew, bread and tea.

THURSDAY

Breakfast: Beef, boiled potatoes, bread and coffee.
Dinner: Roast beef, roasted potatoes, rice soup, bread.
Supper: Potatoes, onion stew, bread and tea.

FRIDAY

Breakfast: Bacon and beans, bread and coffee.
Dinner: Bacon and beans, bean soup and bread.
Supper: Fruit, bread and coffee.

SATURDAY

Breakfast: Beefsteak, boiled potatoes, bread and coffee.
Dinner: Stewed beef with onions, and bread.
Supper: Stew, fruit, bread and coffee.

"The above is the bill of fare throughout the year. Occasionally some extras are had on Sundays and holidays. The rations are supplied in sufficient quantity and always well prepared."

F. S. INGALLS,
Superintendent

tendent Ingalls, who, in his integrity, had the character to keep Manuella in close and segregated confinement.

One of the early superintendents, Superintendent Gates, drew up and published Rules and Regulations for the Prison. Every regulation of its 47 pages reflects a tremendous humanity coupled with an equally unswerving determination to carry out the mission of a maximum security penitentiary, that is, the safe and healthful confinement to the convicts entrusted to its charge. Superintendent Gates was liked and respected by the prisoners and the staff because of the fair rules fairly administered, and because of other reforms.

Neither funds, facilities nor space permitted great experimentation in the development of penitentiary procedures involving reformation, education, and recreation. Honest men in those days had little time for, and were somewhat suspicious of, these frills. Probably the Governor and the people of the Territory would have been less than enthusiastic about paying good taxes for experimentation in such a dubious area.

Even so, within its limited capabilities, the prison offered a library to its inmates, almost from the time it opened its doors. It wasn't until about 1893 that the library amounted to much, but it was open to all, and its use was encouraged. It grew to over 2,000 bound volumes and many periodicals, and first was housed in a case in the north wall, and then in its own building.

There were no formal school facilities, but the prisoners were allowed to form classes and taught such subjects as reading, writing, languages, manual arts, etc. Space for classes was provided, originally in the library cave.

The food was good and without any contemporary criticism, which is quite remarkable. What the prisoners actually thought of the food we can only guess. However, contemporary writers as well as the Superintendents reported that the food was good, wholesome, and abundant, and there is no contrary testimony.

Prison stables, almost at cliff edge overlooking Colorado River. (APHS)

From left to right are the Prison Office and the two-story Guards' Quarters. These were used after the Prison closed to house the High School. (YTPM)

We cannot leave the subject of the Arizona Territorial Prison without touching on the fundamental problem of employing prisoners for their own improvement and the profit of the institution. This is a problem that has been shared by all penitentiaries, everywhere, since 1790. The answer has still not been found. It was not found at the Territorial Prison, but from the Governor down to the working Prison Staff, and from 1876 to 1909, they tried.

A number of projects were considered that never materialized, but there were always several programs going.

The contract labor program previously mentioned was a brief experiment.

The Federal Government presented the Territory with 2,115 acres of Gila River bottom land for a farm, but the farm was never successful. In the wet season it was under water, and in the dry season it was too far from water. On the rare occasions when there was a crop, it was almost certain to be flooded out. In terms of the expense of seed, implements, manpower, and results, it was a complete failure.

For a time the Prison wood yard furnished opportunity for labor, and many convicts earned time off their sentences by the hard work in the river bottoms, cutting wood. It had been optimistically hoped that there would be enough such wood to fire the prison boilers, but the stuff burned fast, and it was hardly worth the effort. Eventually it was abandoned.

Blue dirt, a kind of decomposed granite, was found to make a good surface for streets and walkways. The program to mine blue dirt for use both at the prison and for sale was moderately successful, although the financial returns were low.

The prison had a swine yard, and pork was raised for prison consumption. In times of emergency there was substantial demand for large parties of convicts to work on the levees, and after floods to help restore and dig out the town of Yuma.

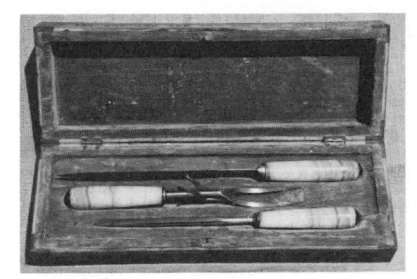

Carving set and case made by one of the prisoners for sale at the Prison. Note the onyx handles. The set is on display at the Prison Museum.

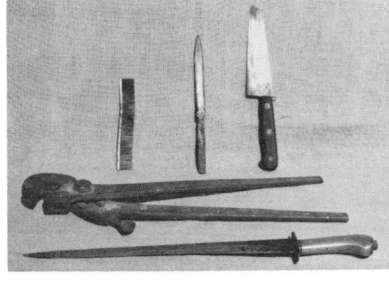

Large wrench used at the Old Pen helps indicate size of comb, stiletto, butcher knife and sword-like knife made by prisoners long dead. These items are all on display at the Prison Museum.

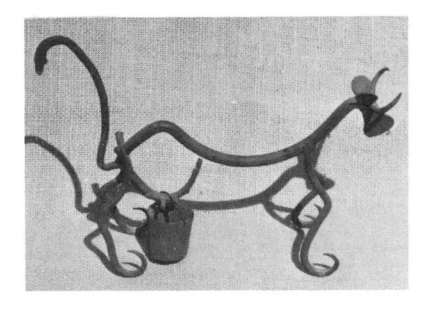

Two canes made by prisoners for sale at the Prison Bazaar with sturdy wheel of prison rock wagon in background, on display at the Museum.

Iron cow, This whimsical and graceful bit of iron work was created and sold by one of the prisoners. It may be seen at the Prison Museum.

Throughout the life of the prison and as required, parties of convicts under armed guard, reconditioned the city streets and Territory highways.

Shops such as the blacksmith shop, electrical repair shop, etc., supplied prison needs and maintained prison equipment. The laundry, bakery, kitchen, office, and stables were important functions.

Clothing and shoe shops for a while supplied garments and shoes to the inmates, as well as to the Territory Insane Asylum at low cost.

Convicts were employed in all the construction work that went on at Prison Hill. However, it was the rock pile, or leveling the rock bank, and excavating into it, that supplied the opportunity for most of the hard labor. In time even this disappeared. First gangs were worked on alternate days, and fewer gangs with fewer men, until the rock pile was only a memory.

In 1904, Superintendent Griffith foreseeing in the future "not too far distant" a complete lack of employment for the prisoners who did not have regularly designated tasks, employed a force of men in making adobes, both for sale and for use in the prison. It was these adobes that made the wall and some of the buildings possible. Two squads of 50 convicts each were employed on the rock bank on alternate days and in building the new wall, and Superintendent Griffith reported that 140 prisoners operated the plant, workshops, kitchen, bake shop, hospital, and various departments of the prison.

One would think that with all this work opportunity there

On display now at the Prison Museum are these two bits and others made by prisoners. Notice the pistol design of the one on the left.

would be "jobs for all." Such was not the case. Both because the greater number of prisoners were unskilled and capable only of common labor, and because there just wasn't enough work even for those who could do it.

It was a private enterprise type of industry that apparently lasted as long as the Prison, which gave all those prisoners with talent and who were "handy" an opportunity to create an occupation to absorb their thought and effort, and a chance of a modest profit. Most of the prisoners made something: jewelry from onyx, braided hatbands and belts, hair and leather bridles, canes, lace, knick-knacks, scrimshaw, and artifacts of all kinds. These they sold in a sort of Bazaar that was open to the public. The prison fund received 25 cents admission charged the visitors, who came from curiosity, and to sell the prisoners their melons and merchandise, and the prison also received one-third of the proceeds of the sales of the merchandise sold by the prisoners. This practice came formally under attack by an investigative committee. No alternatives were suggested to occupy the prisoners' time and thought, and the practice served a useful purpose, so the Bazaar continued up to the time the prison closed. Many beautiful articles, interesting iron work, figures, and jewelry were made, and there are still handsome cabinets in Yuma and Arizona which came from the tools and cabinet shop of the Old Pen.

By this industry the prisoners were able to supply funds for their own needs, and to obtain such necessities as stamps, stationery, and extra tobacco. Two-thirds of the sale proceeds were held for the prisoner, subject to his option to draw small amounts, and in some cases provided a fair stake for the prisoner upon his release.

Only a few ruins remain to suggest the Story of the Arizona Territorial Prison. And in spite of the shock and mental impact that these ruins bring to most visitors, it is a good story.

EPILOGUE

HE history of this much maligned institution on Prison Hill did not end in 1909, although it was never again used as a penitentiary.

The first Yuma Union High School burned while under construction in 1910 and at once some of the prison accommodations and facilities were put to use as a temporary high school. From 1910 to 1914 Yuma's youth swarmed the area which so recently had housed Arizona's bad men. None of the buildings used in this educational program now stand. They included the former Mess Hall and the Hospital over the cell blocks, and shops and other buildings scattered over the little mesa.

Youth easily triumphed over the environment and named their athletic teams the "Crims" or "Criminals," by which names they still are known. Many of Yuma's old timers yet say with pride, "I went to high school at the Old Pen." To be a "warden" meant and means today membership in the honor society.

But when the new Yuma Union High School buildings were completed in 1914 Prison Hill was again abandoned. Actually the abandonment was only official. Hobos and bums traveling the freight trains and the highways found temporary sanctuary there, and as long as they behaved no one bothered them. Prison Hill became "Bums' Hill," and when the depression came in 1929 impoverished families found rent-free accommodations in the cells.

Meanwhile the walls had been leveled and the buildings, one by one, torn down. The hospital burned in 1918 climaxing a drunken hobo celebration.

Front of adobe building inside "New Yard" showing use to which it was put during depression years. The cells in the background are still there. The shower stall on the right has been torn down. (YTPM)

The VFW found a home in the Guards Quarters, occupying this building for many years until it burned down in 1958.

The enterprising Yuma post of the Veterans of Foreign Wars took over the old prison facility and controlled and encouraged tourist traffic. The Old Pen became a VFW Clubhouse, truly at last a "Clubhouse (if not a Country Club) on the Colorado." Many community social functions were held in the old guards' quarters.

After a dispute with this organization concerning the destruction of the high guard tower and the 60,000 gallon reservoir, interest in the decaying institution began to revive. This was encouraged by Yuma people who recognized the historical value and the potential tourist interest of the venerable one-time maximum security prison, the name of which

so long had been a byword among evildoers of the Southwest. Public opinion roused and in 1941 the facility, which had reverted to the City, was made into a Museum.

Official action came too late to prevent much of the theft and cannibalization that had taken place over the years when no responsible citizen indicated much concern over the former prison. The iron cage inside the Dungeon was dismantled and taken to San Luis, Mexico, where it is still in use in the prison there. Other ironwork was taken by several city and county authorities of Arizona to improve their jail facilities and may be still found, if not recognized, scattered about the state.

Mrs. Clarissa Winsor eventually became the first curator, and created a Museum in the restored dining hall. The activity was supported by John Huber, Mayor Walter Ingalls (son of former Superintendent Frank Ingalls), George Robinson, Dr. R. R. Knotts, and other civic-minded Yuma citizens. For 25 years this dedicated, lovely woman, Clarissa Winsor, doggedly persevered in building a facility that eventually, in 1960, was taken over by the Arizona State Parks. By this time the name of the prison had been mutated from The Arizona Territorial Prison, at Yuma, to The Yuma Territorial Prison. It joined the park facilities as second in seniority and perhaps as first in tourist interest. 165,000 visitors now annually inspect the cell blocks and the Museum, each counting the experience as one of the most interesting of his trip.

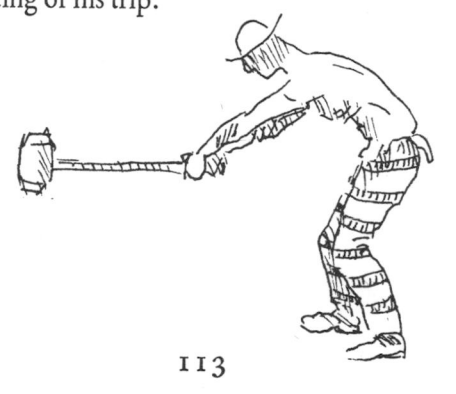

Best wishes. Doe

John Jeffers